COLOUR CODING

ORANGE TREE COURTYARD

THE GIRALDA

NORTH CHAPELS

WEST CHAPELS

SOUTH CHAPELS

EAST CHAPELS

A CATHEDRAL WITHIN THE CATHEDRAL

1 Orange Tree Courtyard
2 The Giralda

NORTH CHAPELS
3 Chapel of Our Lady of the Pillar
4 Chapel of the Evangelists
5 Chapel of the Annunciation
6 Conception Doorway
7 St. Francis' Chapel
8 Chapel of St. James the Apostle
9 Scalas Chapel
10 St. Anthony's Chapel or Baptistery
11 Tabernacle Doorway

WEST CHAPELS
12 Chapel of Las Angustias
13 Baptistery Doorway
14 St. Leandro's Chapel
15 Assumption Doorway
16 St. Isidro's Chapel
17 Nativity Doorway

SOUTH CHAPELS
18 St. Laureano's Chapel
19 Chapel of the Maracaibo Christ
20 St. Joseph's Chapel
21 St. Hermenegild's Chapel
22 Chapel of the Virgin of La Antigua: Chapel of the Hispanic World or Our Lady of the Discovery
23 Prince's Doorway
24 Monument to Christopher Columbus
25 Chapel of the Sorrows
26 Chalice Vestry
27 St. Andrew's Chapel
28 Main Vestry and Chapter House annexes
29 Oils Courtyard
30 Chapter House or Marshal Courtyard
31 Ante-Chapter House
32 Chapter House
33 Former Counting House
34 Marshal Chapel

EAST CHAPELS
35 Campanilla Doorway
36 Chapel of the "Large" Blessed Virgin
37 Royal Chapel: Marian Sanctuary of the City
38 St. Peter's Chapel
39 Palos Doorway

A CATHEDRAL WITHIN THE CATHEDRAL
40 Chancel
41 Choir
42 Chapel of the Blessed Virgin
43 Chapel of the Incarnation
44 Retrochoir
45 Chapel of the Virgin of the Star
46 St. Gregory's Chapel
47 Doorway of Forgiveness

Gift and book–shop

VISITOR'S GUIDE

THE CATHEDRAL
IN
SEVILLE

Juan Guillén Torralba

Legal deposit: M-25030-2003

I.S.B.N.: 84-8003-143-3

Coordination: Aldeasa

Design: Aldeasa

Cover design: A. Ochoa de Zabalegui

Layout: Myriam López Consalvi

Translation: Word Works S.L. (Claire Godfrey)

Photographs: Covadonga de Noriega, Aldeasa, Oronoz

Photomechanics: Lucam

Printed in Spain by: Estudios Gráficos Europeos (Egesa)

TABLE OF CONTENTS

ABOUT THE CATHEDRAL 7

HISTORY 8

CATHEDRAL EXTERIOR 10
Main façade 10
Calle Alemanes façade 11
East end façade 14
South façade 16

ORANGE TREE COURTYARD 18

THE GIRALDA 20

CATHEDRAL INTERIOR 22

NORTH CHAPELS 22
Chapel of our Lady of the Pillar 22
Chapel of the Evangelists 22
Chapel of the Annunciation 23
Conception Doorway 23
St. Francis' Chapel 24
Chapel of St. James the Apostle 24
Scalas Chapel 25
St. Anthony's Chapel or Baptistery 26
Tabernacle Doorway 28

WEST CHAPELS 28
Chapel of Las Angustias 28
St. Leandro's Chapel 28
St. Isidoro's Chapel 30

SOUTH CHAPELS 30
St. Laureano's Chapel 30
Chapel of the Maracaibo Christ 31
St. Joseph's Chapel 33
St. Hermenegild's Chapel 33
Chapel of the Virgin of La Antigua: Chapel of the Hispanic World or our Lady of the Discovery 33

PRINCE'S DOORWAY 38
Monument to Christopher Columbus 38
Clock 40
St. Christopher 40
Chapel of the Sorrows 40
Chalice Vestry 41
St. Andrew's Chapel 42
Main Vestry and annexes 44
Oils Courtyard 50
Chapter House Courtyard or Marshal Courtyard 50
Ante-Chapter House 50
Chapter House 52
Former Counting House 53
Marshal Chapel 54

EAST CHAPELS 55
Chapel of the "Large" Blessed Virgin 56
Royal Chapel: Marian Shrine of the City of Mary 58
St. Peter's Chapel 60
Palos Doorway 61

A CATHEDRAL WITHIN THE CATHEDRAL 62
The Chancel 62
Chancel screens 62
Altarpiece 65
Our Lady of the See 67
The Tabernacle 67
Sanctuary 68
Choir 68
Lectern 68
Organs 68
Porticoes 70
Side chapels: 70
Right-hand side of the cathedral: 70
Chapel of the Blessed Virgin 70
Chapel of the Incarnation 70
Retrochoir 70
Left-hand side of the cathedral: 72
Chapel of the Virgin of the Star 72
St. Gregory's Chapel 72

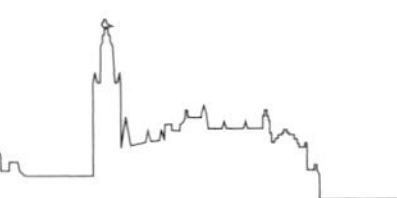

"Let us erect a church so immense that everyone beholding it will take us for madmen".

A mad idea and a colossal task. Seville's cathedral is all things to all men. It is a church for the worshipper, a museum for the artist, an archive for the researcher and a library for the inquisitive mind. Its artistic and documentary wealth consists of a quite stunning collection of paintings and sculptures, precious metalwork and fabrics, documents and books. This successful mingling of Christianity and Islam in one edifice boasts exceptional works from the Gothic, Renaissance, Plateresque and Baroque periods whose notes blend into a unique and incomparable symphony. Together with its tower, the Giralda, the cathedral sums up the very essence of Seville. It is the city's visual image and its great attraction.

ABOUT THE CATHEDRAL

"District A. Quarter 1. Block 13". This is the reference to the cathedral's exact location inscribed on a stone slab set in its main façade. The cathedral,

Aerial view of the cathedral.
Left: the Giralda amidst pinnacles

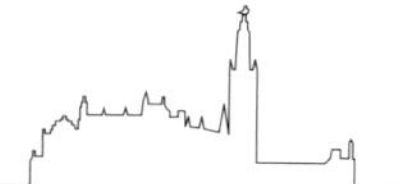

Lantern, exterior view of the dome over the Main Vestry.

Buttresses, flying buttresses, balustrades and pinnacles as seen from outside. Right: the Giralda silhouetted against the Cathedral's architecture.

including the church and its annexes, forms a huge free-standing block in its own right, edged by steps and 157 chained pillars. It follows the same ground plan as the great mosque although the intention of the Christian builders was to take the new church one step further. Measured from east to west, the church is 130.9 metres long inside and 140.5 metres outside. From north to south, its interior and exterior dimensions are 140.7 metres and 161.3 metres respectively. The area occupied by the cathedral totals over 14,500 square metres. A nave and five aisles run lengthways down the interior of the church which is cut across by nine transversal aisles, plus another two forming the chapels. Its width varies between 10 and 16 metres. The interior of the cathedral is vaulted with 70 ojival vaults which take the walls of the chapels and the 32 huge free-standing, eight-sided pillars as their base. The mosque was laid out with 17 aisles divided into eleven bays, punctuated by approximately 160 columns. The heights of the different parts of the cathedral are very much in proportion: the nave and the crossing rise to a height of 35.5 metres, the lantern over the crossing tower reaches 39 metres, the height of the side-aisles is 24 metres and the heights of the chapels are 12.75 metres. The end-result is a rectangular structure, just as in the original mosque. The rather flat east end and shortened transepts which, together with the nave, trace out a Latin cross of the kind found in German Gothic architecture (in the style of a *hallenkirche* or Hall church), are the reason why this cathedral is regarded as the most Nordic of all those in Spain. When the annexes are included in the measurements taken, the complete block making up the cathedral is actually 173.05 metres long by 148.8 metres wide and it occupies a total area of 23,475 square metres. In terms of size, Seville's cathedral is the largest cathedral built in the Gothic style and the third largest church in the world overall, after St. Peter's in Rome and St. Paul's in London. *The Guinness Book of Records* acknowledges it as the cathedral with the biggest surface area in the world, recording its dimensions as 126.18 metres long, 82.6 metres wide and 30.48 metres high. The cathedral in Seville was declared part of World Heritage by UNESCO in 1987. The cathedral in Seville (the Magna Hispalensis), together with the Nobilis Burgensis (Burgos), the Pulchra Leonina (León) and the Dives Toletana (Toledo) represents Gothic architecture in Spain at its very best.

HISTORY

Seville's cathedral was erected on the site of the huge Almohad mosque that had been built on the orders of Caliph Abu Yacub Yusuf (1172-1182). Remains of this great mosque can still be seen in the Patio de Los Naranjos (Orange Tree Courtyard) and in some of the exterior doorways. Two of these, the Puerta del Perdón (Doorway of Forgiveness) and the Lagarto Doorway are still used today. Following the Christian reconquest of Spain from the Moors, the mosque was dedicated as a cathedral and adapted for Christian worship (December 1243). There was no further change until July 8th 1401 when, in the absence of an archbishop for Seville, the canons made one of those mad, sublime decisions that could only have been prompted by the heat of a Sevillian summer:

> In the absence of an archbishop (...) and in the presence of the Dean, Canons, Dignitaries, Prebendaries and companions, they said that since the Church in Seville was in danger of collapsing day by day (...) that another

Baptistery Doorway.

church should be erected and that it should be such a fine church that there would be none to rival it and that it should be in keeping with the grandeur and authority of Seville and its Church as reason commands; and should there not be enough income for the work to be done all those present said that a sum should be taken from the income of each one and that they shall consider this to be a way of serving God; and two Canons were ordered to sign it.

The people of Seville translated this decision into other words so that one of the canons was quoted as having said: "Let us erect a church so immense that everyone beholding it will take us for madmen". Those same clergymen kept their word and almost lived to see the finished work. Construction of the new cathedral started in 1408 and in little more than seventy years it had become a reality. Although many hands were involved in its construction, the cathedral still preserves great unity as the idea prevailed over the ravages of time. It is not known who actually designed it but the very first craftsmen involved in the project that we know of include Alonso Martínez and Pedro García, as well as artisans from abroad like Isambret, Carlin and Juan Norman. Juan de Hoces was the master builder between 1478 and 1496. Simon of Cologne may have built the lantern over the crossing tower (the one he built in Burgos Cathedral collapsed, 1495-1498) although some people attribute it to Alonso Rodríguez (1496-1513). The Gothic work was completed by Juan Gil de Hontañón (1513-1519). The last stone was laid in place on October 10th 1506 and on March 11th the following year the cathedral was finished. The lantern collapsed in December of 1511 and its reconstruction prompted the Renaissance redesign on which such illustrious master builders as Diego de Riaño (1528-1534), Martín de Gaínza (1534-1556), Hernán Ruiz the Younger (1557-1569), Pedro Díaz Palacios (1569-1574), Juan de Maeda (1574-1576) and Asensio de Maeda (1576-1602) all worked. The end-result bears witness to their craftsmanship and skill.

St. Michael's or Nativity Doorway.

CATHEDRAL EXTERIOR

Main façade. Standing on Avenida de la Constitución, the most cosmopolitan of all of Seville's thoroughfares, the main façade hints at the interior structure of a nave and four aisles, plus side chapels, and makes no attempt to conceal its supporting flying buttresses. There are three doorways on this side of the building: San Miguel (St. Michael's Doorway), Asunción (Assumption Doorway) and Bautisterio (Baptistry Doorway). The side doorways are the oldest (Carlin, 15th century). The tympana of all three doorways are decorated in relief: the *Nativity* is depicted on St. Michael's Doorway, the *Baptising of Jesus* can be seen above the Baptistery Doorway and the *Assumption* is featured above the door bearing the same name. The oldest sculptures (Mercadante of Brittany and Pedro Millán, 15th century) are made of polychrome fired clay (pottery, of course, has always been a traditional craft practised in Seville), adding a splash of colour to doors that are all one colour now. Even though it only dates from the last century (designed by Fernando Rosales and decorated by Ricardo Bellver), the main doorway is not at all out of keeping with the rest of the façade. The *Sagrario* (Tabernacle)

Church, for which construction started in 1618, follows on from the Gothic structure.

Calle Alemanes façade. The crenellated wall with its lower buttresses gives away its Almohad past. Another Almohad element is the Puerta del Perdón (Doorway of Forgiveness), which used to be the most important door

Exterior of Doorway of Forgiveness and detail of the Christ of Forgiveness.

Following the Christian reconquest of Seville under Ferdinand III in 1248, the city's mosque was dedicated as a cathedral to St. Mary although its original structure was preserved until the 15th century when the Chapter ordered it to be demolished to make way for the construction of the building still on the site today. A number of Almohad elements were kept and integrated into the new cathedral. The Doorway of Forgiveness, once the main entrance into the mosque, is one such example.

Top and right: Assumption Doorway. Bottom: Campanilla Doorway. Facing page: Western façade.

into the *sahn* or *Ablutions Courtyard* and led into the main entrance to the mosque, laid out north to south. Although alterations have been made to it since then, the door still retains its original Islamic charm. Indeed, the two leaves made of bronze-coated cedar wood are the original pieces of that door. They measure 9 metres by 2 metres and are decorated with vegetal motifs and

Christ's entry into Jerusalem, *Campanilla Doorway tympanum. Right: the Giralda as seen from the Plaza del Triunfo.*

"Giralda in pure prism of Seville,/balanced out of lead and the star,/cast in a blue setting, flawless tower,/seedless palm of architecture (...)/Against the light of the lemon tree moon,/your edge is bevelled, a barber's blade/ refining its most beautiful vertical line./Touch slides its futile caress./As mudéjar I love you, not Christian./Volume and nothing else: base and height".
(Gerardo Diego)

Kufic lettering. The door-knockers, however, are copies of the originals now on display inside the cathedral. They are shaped like Almohad palms and seem to be edged in bronze with inscriptions taken from the Koran. The metal was entirely hand-engraved. Flanking the doorway itself are two huge terracotta sculptures of *St. Peter* and *St. Paul* and two further carvings depicting the *Angel and Mary* in the Annunciation. There is also a relief carving of the *Expulsion of the merchants* (Miguel Florentín, 1519-1522). The entrance hall contains a small altarpiece with an Ecce Homo, or Christ of Forgiveness (18th century), whence the door takes its name. The door leading into the **cathedral's Christopher Columbus Library** is on the corner of Calle Alemanes and Placentines. Cervantes used these steps as the site for episodes in his short novel *Rinconete y Cortadillo*: Monopodio, one of the characters in the novel, supposedly had an academy close to this spot.

East end façade. The original Almohad structure ending at the Puerta del Lagarto (Crocodile Doorway) continues on from the corner to the tower. The Giralda brings together the Muslim and the Gothic styles. The east end is slotted between two of Seville's most intimate squares with their dedication to the Virgin Mary: Virgen de los Reyes and Triunfo (Inmaculada). This particular

View of the Orange Tree Courtyard from the Giralda.

façade has two Gothic doorways. The Puerta de los Palos (Palos Doorway) is notable for the beautiful face of the Virgin in the *Adoration of the Magi* decorating its tympanum. The scene set above Campanilla (Little bell) Doorway is *Christ's entry into Jerusalem*. These two reliefs are surrounded by fired clay figures of prophets and saints (M. Florentín, 16th century). The apse of the Royal Chapel (1520-1523) projects out between the two doorways.

South façade. This side of the building rubs shoulders with the Palacio de la Diputación (provincial government headquarters) and the aristocratic Alcázar fortress walls, the Puerta del León (Lion Door) and the entrance arch to its Patio de Banderas courtyard. It also stands alongside the elegant Lonja building which was constructed by Juan de Herrera as a Sevillian version of El Escorial and has now been turned into the Archive of the Indies. In the centre is the monument to the Blessed Virgin. Viewed from this side, the cathedral is a breathtakingly beautiful sight with its mass of flying buttresses, pinnacles, spires and stone balustrades that only serve to heighten the grandeur and symmetry of its overall structure. It must be one of the most classical and alluring corners in the whole world as the Emperor Charles V acknowledged at the time.
The only door on this side of the building is the Puerta de San Cristóbal (St. Christopher's Doorway), otherwise known as the *Puerta del Príncipe*

"Seville's Cathedral, that huge fortress of the Catholic faith, hangs its bells in the Muslim Giralda and preserves at its very heart its Arab Orange Tree Courtyard."
(Marguerite Yourcenar)

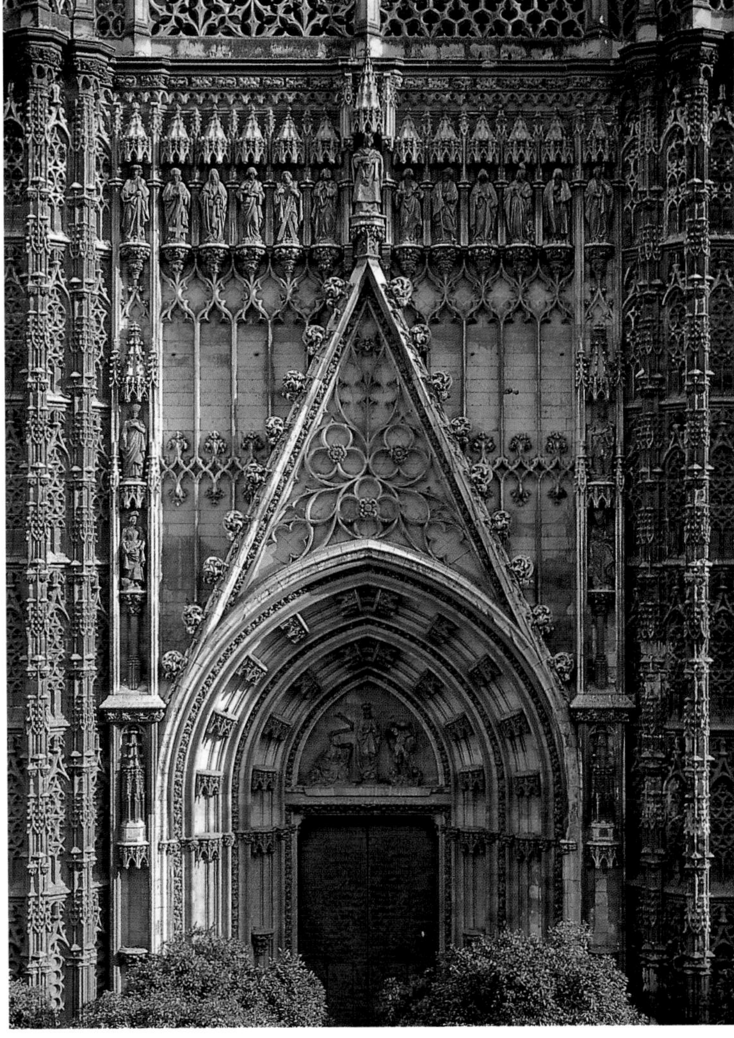

Conceptión Doorway.

(Prince's Doorway) as this is the entrance used by monarchs because of its proximity to the Alcázar. The doorway is recessed somewhat on account of the position of the Renaissance portion of the building. The doorway was designed by Demetrio de los Ríos and was built under the supervision of Alfonso Fernández Casanova (1887-1895).

Seville's Cathedral, that huge fortress of the Catholic faith, hangs its bells in the Muslim Giralda and preserves at its very heart its Arab Orange Tree Courtyard (Marguerite Yourcenar).

"The Doorway of Forgiveness leads into the Orange Tree Courtyard -with its orange trees and the scent of its now long-gone palms and cypress trees still hanging in the air-, the most peaceful spot in the whole of Spain in the words of the Venetian ambassador Andrés Navagero (...). Two doorways lead into the Cathedral from the Orange tree Courtyard: Conception Doorway and the Puerta del Lagarto ("Crocodile" Doorway) which lies at the end of the Lagarto or Pomegranate Cloister underneath the magnificent Christopher Columbus library."
(Camilo José Cela: *Primer viaje andaluz*)

Giralda, detail of central section. Right: uppermost section of the Giralda from the Azucenas Balcony. Facing page: Cathedral and Giralda from the Patio de Banderas courtyard.

The Giralda

The Tower sleeps standing up
and the Cathedral lying down
because the Giralda is life
and the Cathedral is faith.
From the square behold
the bells flying through the air
as they await the time for evening prayer.
And on their own, without a ringer
the bells wag their steel tongues
and awaken St. Ferdinand.

(Fernando Villalón)

ORANGE TREE COURTYARD

The Almohad origin of this oasis of peace and tranquillity in the heart of the city is patent right from the very entrance to it: the doorway, the remains of the pillars from the mosque, the enclosing wall, the *Lagarto* aisle bay with its sloped

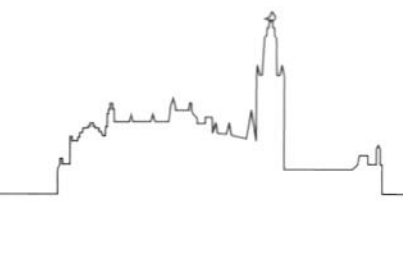

Central screen viewed from the high altar.

galleries, the basin for ablutions (albeit Roman in origin). The cathedral's archive, the **Chapter library and the Christopher Columbus library** (a source of great pride to the chapter) are located between the Lagarto and Forgiveness doorways. **The Chapel of Our Lady of the Pomegranate** containing Visigothic capitals is right next to the door. There are a whole host of anecdotes connected with the courtyard. For instance, in October 1498, the illustrious Spanish grammarian and humanist Antonio de Nebrija applied for a licence to teach grammar in the Pomegranate chapel and the order was issued by the chapter "to have it decked out with benches and matting as required". The venerable Contreras, St. Vicente Ferrer and St. Francisco de Borja, to name but a few examples, all preached from the tiny pulpit backing onto the nave. Hanging in the bay are the famous *Lagarto* (crocodile), an elephant's tusk, a stick and a bit. They may have been gifts, votive offerings or symbols. It does not really matter. On the wall hangs a painting of Christ known as the "*Christ of the brooms*" because his lamp was kept burning with the money swept up in the rubbish. All of these elements add up to a spot that is brimming with atmosphere: the symmetrical layout of the orange trees, the interior of the Almohad doors, the view of the Giralda which seems to be loftier than ever when seen from this courtyard, memories of sermons and classes taught by Nebrija, and of the street-cleaners with their brooms who would try to keep an oil lamp lit at the feet of the figure of Christ on the Cross.

Two doorways provide access to the cathedral from this courtyard. The huge Puerta de la Concepción (Conception Doorway) (Adolfo Fernández Casanova, 1895-1927) imitates ancient models The scene depicted in its tympanum is the *Blessed Virgin, St. Michael* and *St John the Evangelist* with *Jesus and the apostles* up above. The sculptures were carved by Joaquín Bilbao, Adolfo López and Eduardo Muñoz. The simpler, dignified Puerta de la Granada (Pomegranate Doorway) welcomes all those that pass through it with the scene of *Our Lady of Repose with David and Solomon* (Mercadante or Pedro Millán, 15th century).

THE GIRALDA

The Giralda is a multifaceted metaphor. It is an Islamic minaret designed in stone and completed in brick, the strong tower that was converted to Christianity, a pedestal for faith to stand on and the symbol of the city.

The mosque was barely finished when Ben Basso began construction of the tower (1184) and the Almohad victory over Alfonso VIII (Alarcos, 1195) provided the impetus for its completion (Ali de Gomara, 1198). It was originally topped by an upper storey bearing four gilded spheres (the *yamur*). The tower was destroyed in the earthquake that hit the city on August 24th 1356 and brilliantly redesigned subsequently by Hernán Ruiz the Younger (1558-1568). The Giraldillo bronze figure-weather vane was cast at the same time. Studies conducted in 1987 have since revealed that this enormous tower is actually built on foundations that run to a depth of just a few metres.

Lantern tower area and stained glass windows in the wings of the crossing. Right-hand page: vaulting over the choir and organ.

The tower rises to a height of 93.9 metres and is split vertically into three separate panels on its outer structure. The central section holds the window openings and the two panels on either side of it are decorated with diamond shapes carved in brick. A gently sloping ramp leads up to the belfry where steps continue on right up to the very top of the building. The Renaissance belfry is formed by a lower section housing the bells themselves which is topped by four

Our Lady of the Pillar.

flower pots of lilies and decorated with relief carvings of heads. The storey above that is the *Clock* section. A frieze runs around it on which the words TURRIS-FORTISSIMA-NOMEN DÑI-PROV.18 are inscribed and there are more relief carvings. The *Stars* section comes next with faces depicting the winds and above it is the *Balls* section holding up the cupola, the *Pitcher* and the pedestal on which the *Giraldillo* bronze weather-vane stands. A replica of the Giraldillo is on display inside the cathedral.

CATHEDRAL INTERIOR

> "It is all so severe and majestic, almost as if we had gone out of the real world and into a gigantic grotto that had been put together by a giant who adored geometry, symmetry and order" (Fernando Chueca Goitia).

Visitors to the cathedral are overwhelmed by its grandeur into a feeling of insignificance and into a state of devoted absorption by the semi-darkness. The silence is truly powerful. The light flickers and quivers, creating that special atmosphere that so enthralled the Romantics. A total of 81 stained glass windows making up what may be the most comprehensive and interesting collection of its kind in Spain filter and reflect Seville's own luminosity. They include works by artists such as Arnao de Vergara, Arnao of Flanders, Charles of Bruges, Vicente Menardo and Jean Jacques (15th-16th century), together with some more modern examples.

NORTH CHAPELS

St. Jude, *in the Chapel of Our Lady of the Pillar, a very special devotion.*

Chapel of Our Lady of the Pillar. This particular chapel dates back to the time of the old mosque-cathedral when it was founded by members of the Aragonese nobility. The statue of *Our Lady of the Pillar* carved in polychrome terracotta is possibly the most successful work executed by Pedro Millán (1500). Elegantly formed, the figure radiates nobility and refinement, dignity and mysticism. The figure of the Infant Jesus smiles as he blesses those beholding him. This chapel has become very popular with worshippers over recent years on account of the image of *St. Jude* standing on the altar on the right-hand side of the chapel.

A beautiful stained glass window (1) by Arnao of Flanders depicting *Christ's entry into Jerusalem* can be seen above this chapel.

Chapel of the Evangelists. The beautiful interior stained glass window (2), *Nativity* (Arnao of Flanders, 1553), is matched by the equally fine paintings on board by Hernando de Esturmio (16th century) of which there are nine in total. *St. Gregory's Mass* hangs in the centre below *The Resurrection* and is flanked by the *Evangelists*; *St. Catherine and St. Barbara* are over the altar; *St. Sebastian, St. John the Baptist* and *St. Antony Abbot;* and *Saints Justa and Rufina with the Giralda* as it was before Hernán Ruiz's reform. The purity and perfection of the lines drawn and the colours used are quite striking. Some of the pieces of the choir that is set up for use on Maundy Thursday and Corpus Christi are exhibited here: huge lecterns to hold the choir music, large candlesticks to transport the candles etc., crafted in gilded, polychrome wood with floral decorations and little angels (18th century).

Stop to admire the stained glass window (3) by Arnao of Flanders (1554) above the iron screen. It represents *Lazarus raised from death*.

Above left: parts of the portable choir in the Chapel of the Evangelists. Above right: The placing of the chasuble on St. Idelfonso, *by Valdés Leal, St. Francis' Chapel.*

Chapel of the Annunciation. The stained glass window (4) mingles the *Annunciation* with *Our Lady protector of maidens* (A. de Vergara, 1534). The relevance of the subject chosen is that this particular chapel was once used by a foundation (16th century) that gave dowries to young women of marriageable age. The *Annunciation* appears yet again in the altarpiece (José Rivera, 1771). The real treasures of the chapel, however, are the paintings on board that formed part of the original altarpiece (Cristóbal de Morales, 15th-16th century). They are *Handing over dowries,* the *Donor and his coat of arms, St. Jerome and St. Gregory, St. Bartholomew, St. Peter, St. Thomas and St. James the Lesser, St Ambrose and St Augustine* and a *Calvary*. The *Saviour* in the centre is a later work. There are two iron screens enclosing this chapel, both of which are impressive. The screen to be seen along the side of the chapel is topped by an embossed iron version of the *Annunciation*.

Above the chapel is a stained glass window (5) by A. de Vergara, *Mary Magdalene anointing the feet of Christ* (1554).

Conception Doorway. The painting hanging under the rose window is the *Allegory of the Proclamation of the dogma of the Immaculate Conception against a Sevillian background* (Alfonso Grosso, 1966). Two symmetrical altars can be seen on either side of the door. On the right is the *Assumption of Mary* (Gregorio Ferrari, 18th century), on the left-hand altar is the lovely *Virgin of Bethlehem*, one of the most beautiful works by Alonso Cano (1635). Above it is the *Holy Trinity* (Virgilio Mattoni, 1901). The painting hanging on the left-hand wall is *The slaughter of the Holy Innocents*, thought to be by Jacopo Fardella (17th century).

This is a good spot from which to admire the stained glass windows in this wing: *The Ascension* (6) (1539) above the door and *The Resurrection* (7) (Charles of Bruges, 1558) and several of *Apostles and Saints* (8) (Arnao of Flanders, executed between 1543 and 1551) on the window side.

Sepulchre of Archbishop Gonzalo de Mena, *Chapel of St. James the Apostle.*

Archbishop Mena's sepulchre was carved between 1401 and 1421 on the instructions of the Cathedral Chapter by an unknown, brilliant artist whose technique reveals Italian influences. In the late 16th century, it was moved to the Santa María de las Cuevas monastery the prelate had founded in 1400 before being returned to the Cathedral in 1837, following the period of seizure of church property (known as the *Desamortización*)

St. Francis' Chapel. St. Francis of Assisi is extolled in the magnificent stained glass window (9) entitled the *Ecstasy* (Arnao of Flanders, 1554) and in the altarpiece (Bernardo Simón de Pineda, 1661) where the impressive canvas depicting the *Apotheosis* (1656) can be admired as "one of the best works by Francisco de Herrera el Mozo [the Younger], on account of its fanciful composition, mellow, diffused colouring, red and transparent inks and the fine contrast in the way light and dark are painted (Ceán Bermúdez). Above it hangs *The placing of the chasuble on St. Ildelfonso* (Valdés Leal, 1661), an excellent example of realism and careful composition. A small altarpiece featuring *St. Teresa* (17th century), a bust of Ecce Homo and several other paintings complete the contents of the chapel.

The stained glass window (10) illustrates *St. Francis surrounded by saints of his order* (E. Alemán, 1478).

Chapel of St. James the Apostle. This is really a tiny, heterogeneous museum. There is a splendid iron screen, a stained glass window (11) depicting *The conversion of St Paul* (Vicente Menardo, 1560) and a magnificent altarpiece embellished with angels and vegetal motifs (B.S. de Pineda, 1663). There is also a

monumental canvas of *St. James at the Battle of Clavijo* (Juan de Roelas) with *The martyrdom of St. Lawrence* (Valdés Leal, 1663) hanging above it. A Pietà stands on top of the altar plinth itself (Sevillian school, 16th century). The chapel also boasts a collection of fifteen paintings on board which used to form part of the old altarpiece-reliquary from the Main Vestry (Antón Pérez, 1547-1548).

There are still two more treasures to be admired here: two outstanding sculptures that are very different but both beautiful in their own right. Firstly, the magnificent *sepulchre of the Archbishop of Seville Gonzalo de Mena* (1394-1401), a Gothic work in alabaster with scenes from the Gospels carved in relief on the front and side panels, including the side placed up against the wall. The carved figure of the archbishop reclines atop the tomb-chest. The other sculpture is a relief crafted in glazed clay and known as Our Lady of the Cushion. The Infant Jesus plays with his Mother Mary's veil. Seated on a cushion, Mary tenderly caresses her Son's naked foot (Andrea dell Robbia's studio, 15th-16th century). The most outstanding characteristics of this sculpture are Mary's beautiful features, the gestures of the Infant Jesus, the composition and the soft colouring used.

Above the chapel is a stained glass window depicting *Saints Justa and Rufina* (12), *St. James and St. Barbara* (13) (E. Alemán, 1478).

Scalas Chapel. Here we have a delightful Renaissance iron screen with *The Virgin and the apostles* in wrought iron (1564), a stained glass window featuring the *Coming of the Holy Spirit and two canons* (1880) and the marble tomb-chest of *Baltasar del Río*, canon and archdeacon of Niebla, a relation of Pope Julius II and Pope Leo X and Bishop of Scalas. A catafalque bears the reclining figure of the chapel founder, borne by two little angels holding cartouches and adorned with Our Lady of Comfort, a beautiful medallion in relief at the back, flanked by St. Peter and St. Paul. The majestic altarpiece stands in the gallery above it. It is divided into three vertical sections by two Plateresque columns which picture the

Top: Our Lady of the Pomegranate and the Mausoleum of Bishop Don Baltasar del Río, *Scalas Chapel. Bottom:* Our Lady of the Cushion *in the Chapel of St. James the Apostle.*

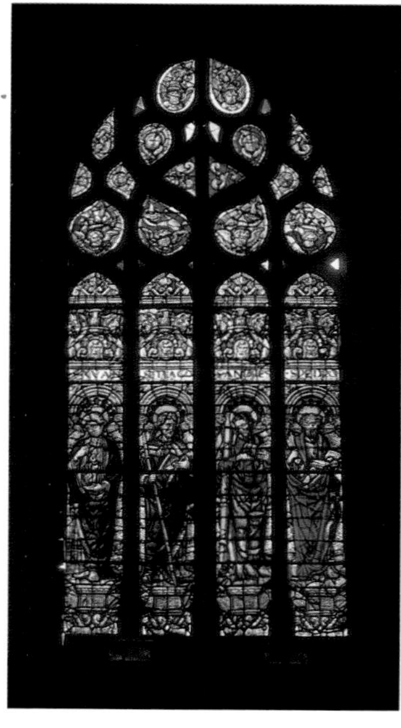

Stained glass window with four apostles in the crossing and font in St. Anthony's Chapel. Right-hand page: general view of Scalas Chapel.

bishop and his coat of arms on their pedestals. On the altar is a bas-relief illustrating *The Miracle of the Loaves and the Fishes* below the outstanding composition *The Coming of the Holy Spirit* with its well-executed figures. At the very top is a bust of the *Heavenly Father worshipped by two angels.* The mausoleum is actually empty as the bishop was eventually buried in Rome. The monument is Italian and was erected on May 5th 1539. There used to be a doorway leading out of this chapel into the Orange Tree Courtyard with a door (which has been preserved) designed by Hernán Ruiz or Pedro de Riaño.

On the opposite wall is yet another artistic gem: *Our Lady of the Pomegranate.* This lovely terracotta by Lucca della Robbia depicts the Virgin Mary surrounded by saints and crowned by angels as she offers the Infant Jesus a pomegranate (14th-15th century).

The stained glass window above the chapel (15) is by E. Alemán (1478) and represents *Four apostles.*

St. Anthony's Chapel or Baptistery. Light filters into this chapel through a stained glass window (16) picturing *Saints Justa and Rufina and the Saint of the Chapel* (Juan Bautista de León, 1685). Viewed from the transversal aisle, the Renaissance font decorated with angels around its base and vegetal motifs fringing the basin almost seems to be holding up the huge frame (Pineda, 1668) with two masterpieces by Murillo (the *Vision of St. Anthony* (1656) and *The Baptising of Jesus* (1668). In spite of its size (5.6 x 3.75 m) the Vision of St. Anthony is a surprisingly intimate work. The saint is lost in his own thoughts as he watches the heavens open and God descend as a child amidst angels. A typical monk's table in the foreground and a cloister visible in the distance provide the monastic setting for

The oldest stained glass windows in the Cathedral were made between 1478 and 1483 by Enrique Alemán, a German-born craftsman whose style reveals his background training in workshops in the Alsace and a marked Flemish influence.

Our Lady of the Tree Strawberry.

the scene. The simplicity and gentle emotion of the subject matter, added to the clever interplay of light and shadow, make this painting one of the most admired works by the Seville-born painter. The other painting by Murillo is of a similarly high standard and is in keeping with the chapel's sacramental purpose.

The finishing touch to this beautiful chapel is a horizontal beam comprising 18 paintings on board portraying *Apostles, prophets and saints and the Pietà* (16th century). This work has been carefully restored so that the clearly-drawn lines and strength of the faces depicted can be appreciated together with their original colouring. Other important works are: *Blessed Virgin* (Juan de Roelas), *St. Peter before the Lord and St. Peter in prison* (Valdés Leal) and two paintings representing the *Creation* (Simón de Vos).

The stained glass window (17) above the chapel (E. Alemán, 1478) is of *The Four Evangelists*.

Tabernacle Doorway. Opened in 1682, it is embellished with statues of the patron saints (*St. Ferdinand, St. Leandro and St. Isidoro, Saints Justa and Rufina)* and provides the backcloth for a reproduction of the Giraldillo as the weather vane topping the belfry is commonly known. A women symbolises the Catholic Church triumphing over heresy and over the Turks following an idea by the canon and humanist Francisco Pacheco. Bartolomé Morel cast it between 1566 and 1568 (August 13th). It measures 7.52 m from the base of the ball to the cross.

WEST CHAPELS

Chapel of Las Angustias (Distress). In the painting by Juan de Roelas (1609), Mary takes up her lifeless son against a dark background. She is accompanied by St. John and Mary Magdalene. Angels with symbols of the Passion hold up the spiral columns in the altarpiece. The *Holy Face of Christ* can be seen up above between *Faith and Hope*.

Visitation Altar. An unrivalled collection of paintings on board by Pedro Villegas Marmolejo, one of the great Sevillian painters, is on display in this chapel. The painter's signature is visible on the central panel, *The Visitation of Mary to St. Elizabeth*. Flanking it are *St. Blas, The Baptising of Christ, St. James and St. Sebastian. Portraits of the Donor and his relations* can be seen above the altar, with the *Infant Jesus bathed in glory* (1566) portrayed in the uppermost central panel. The outstanding features of this painting are the perfectly drawn figures, their fine forms and the mellow, fresh colours. On top of the altar is a high relief of *Penitent St. Jerome* (Jerónimo Hernández, 1566), an extremely fine naturalistic figure. The iron screen dates from 1568.

The stained glass window (18) set above the Baptistery Doorway is a Renaissance work by Vicente Menardo (1568), the *Visitation*.

Altar to the Virgin of La Alcobilla. A *Pietà* sculptural group in polychrome fired clay reveals its Flemish influences (14th century).

St. Leandro's Chapel. It has an elaborately carved stone portal, a Baroque iron screen and an altarpiece with spiral columns (1730). *St. Leandro* is in the centre with *St. Fulgencio and St. Antony Abbot; St. Dominic* is in the centre at the very top (Duque Cornejo, 1734). There are also two canvases illustrating episodes from the life of St. Leandro (J. Mausola, 1735).

Altar of the Christ Child. This charming image made in polychrome wood is from Martínez Montañés' school (16th century). It is commonly known as

Lorenzo Mercadante of Brittany's name first appeared amongst the artisans working on Seville's Cathedral in 1454 as the sculptor of an image of the Virgin identified by some authors as Our Lady of the Tree Strawberry. This fine alabaster carving reveals the unmistakable style of the craftsman from Brittany. It can now be seen with its original polychrome features following painstaking restoration work carried out in 1983.

Left: Dumb Child. *Above:* Our Lady of the Ribbon.

The Dumb Child because of the way the figure is pursing his lips and is popular as a subject of worship.

Altar of Comfort. In the centre is *The Virgin with the Christ Child between St. James the Greater and St. Anthony,* painted on Gothic board (Alonso M. de Tovar, 1720). *The Donor* is at their feet.

Between 1454 and 1467, the probable date of his death, Lorenzo Mercadante of Brittany worked on the sculptures adorning the Cathedral in Seville. His figures were mostly crafted in terracotta, unglazed fired clay. He was an expert in this technique which is exemplified here in the exquisite *Our Lady of the Ribbon.*

St. Isidoro's Chapel.

Stained glass windows. A rose window (19) (2.8 m in diameter) depicts the *Evangelists* (20) (Vicente Menardo, 1566). A window overlooking the aisle represents characters from the Bible (21) (E. Alemán, 1478-1483).

Christopher Columbus's son is buried between the retrochoir and the door. Hernández Colón (Colombus) was one of the greatest bibliophiles ever to have lived. He bequeathed his library to the cathedral. He died in July 1539.

A Calvary sculptural group can be seen hanging over the main door. It was crafted by Francisco Antonio Girón and used as the crowning element of the Maundy Thursday great monument.

Silver Altar. The huge silver altar attached to the inside of the main door is erected from Maundy Thursday until Corpus Christi. This work by Juan Laureano de Piano and Mateo Gutiérrez (1688-1690) comprises numerous busts and statues of saints, topped by a huge sun and a crown. The urn holding the gold ciborium with the Eucharist is in the centre.

Altar of the Guardian Angel. This is one of the most evocative works by Murillo (1665) illustrating the idea of the Angel who watches over man portrayed as a child.

Altar of Our Lady of the Tree Strawberry. This is an intimate scene in which Mother Mary offers her breast to the Child Christ whose gaze rests on the onlooker whilst a kneeling angel offers him a basket of tree strawberries. This alabaster ensemble is by Lorenzo Mercadante of Brittany (15th century). Rising to a height of 1.20 metres, the facial expressions of the figures and the way their clothing hangs are particularly well-sculpted. *The Scourging of Christ* stands atop the altarpiece.

St. Isidoro's Chapel. It matches the chapel of St. Leandro with its elaborately carved portal, beautiful iron screen (17th century) and polychrome plasterwork in its interior. The altarpiece with its spiral columns (B. Simón de Pineda, 1662-1664) is the frame for four anonymous images: *St. Isidro*, flanked by *St. Francis* and *St. Diego of Alcalá* with *St. Ferdinand* appearing in the attic.

Altar of Our Lady of the Ribbon. This is another jewel of a sculpture by Mercadante of Brittany, made in polychrome fired clay. A full-length figure of the *Virgin Mary* holds Christ her Son in her arms. Their faces are highly expressive. Mary is wrapped in a cloak and her tunic is fastened with a ribbon which hangs in charming fashion. The Christ Child is holding a book. The work is dated between 1460 and 1470.

A stained glass window (22) depicting *The Annunciation* overlooks the Puerta de San Miguel or St. Michael's Doorway. It is a Renaissance work by Vicente Menardo (1566)

Altar of the Nativity. A Plateresque iron screen (16th century) encloses an altarpiece consisting of paintings by Luis de Vargas who Francisco Pacheco once called "the light of painting and a worthy father of art in his homeland of Seville". In the centre is the *Adoration of the shepherds*. At the sides: *Annunciation, Presentation, St. John, St. Luke, St. Matthew, St. Mark* and *the Adoration of the Magi.*

Altarpiece in St. Laureano's Chapel.

SOUTH CHAPELS

St. Laureano's Chapel. According to tradition, this saint was once Archbishop of Seville. The stained glass window (23) testifies to the fact with its

Left: Cardinal de la Lastra's sepulchre.
Right: Maracaibo Christ.

illustration of *St. Laureano, St. Isidoro and St. Leandro* (Vicente Menardo, 1572). Although it is true, as Ceán Bermúdez said, that "the first stone was placed in this chapel when work on the cathedral began and as it was the first chapel to be completed religious services were held in this chapel whilst the rest of the church was being built", everything contained in this chapel actually dates from the 18th century. The altarpiece depicts *St. Laureano* and various scenes taken from his life. His *Martyrdom* depicted in relief is in the upper part alongside angels with orles. The *paintings with scenes from the life of the Saint* are by the Sevillian painter Matías de Arteaga (1700-1702). The frames, altarpiece and figures were crafted by the same anonymous hand. The chapel is the burial place of a number of dignitaries but only the *mausoleum of Cardinal D. Joaquín Lluch y Garriga* (1877-882) is actually visible. The figure of the archbishop at prayer is mounted on a rostrum decorated with angels and coats of arms (Agapito Vallmitjana, 1885). The stained glass window (24) above this chapel representing various female *Saints* is by E. Alemán.

Chapel of the Maracaibo Christ. The stained glass window (25) inside the chapel depicts *The Holy Family* (1798). Opposite it is an altarpiece by Joaquín Bilbao (1914) bearing a beautiful painting of *Christ on the Cross* which belonged to one of the original chapels (16th century). Modern bas-reliefs of the *Virgin and St. John* can be seen on either side. This particular work is worshipped under the name of the Maracaibo Christ as it is commonly known. Over on the left-hand wall, mounted on a gallery fronted by a railing, is an altarpiece of paintings on wood (15th century). *St. Bartholomew* is in the centre beside *St. Blas and St. Nicholas, St. James and St. Sebastian*. The

Ricardo Bellver y Ramón (1845-1924) was a member of a prolific dynasty of Valencian-born sculptors. He conducted most of his work in Madrid but was also involved in the completion of the façade of the Cathedral in Seville and was given the commission to craft the praying figure on Cardinal de la Lastra's sepulchre.

Above: St. James the Lesser *in St. Hermenegild's Chapel.*
Right: altarpiece in St. Joseph's Chapel.

The statue of St. James the Lesser was the sole survivor when the Cathedral's original lantern tower collapsed in 1511 due to its excessive height. All the other polychrome stone statues of prophets, apostles and saints adorning the lantern tower were lost.

upper section of the altarpiece above these works bears a sculpture of the *Virgin Mary with the Christ Child* (16th century), flanked by *St. John the Baptist, St. Anne, St. Martha and St. Michael.* Lower down are five paintings of the Passion and a *Crucifixion* appears in the centre. These have all been recently restored and can now be appreciated in their full glory.

On the right is the *tomb of Cardinal D. Luis de la Lastra y Cuesta* (1862-1876), executed in marble. The prelate is kneeling down, clothed in a chasuble, with the mitre of his office at his feet. Angels and coats of arms embellish the corners of the monument (Ricardo Bellver, 1880).

The stained glass window (26) above this chapel depicts *Four Female Saints* (E. Alemán, 1478).

St. Joseph's Chapel. There is a modern interior stained glass window (27) representing *The Nativity* (1932). The marble altarpiece is Neo-Classical in style (18th century) and bears the figure of *St. Joseph* executed in polychrome wood (José Esteve Bonet) in the centre. In the foreground is *the mausoleum and sarcophagus cover of Cardinal Bueno Monreal* (1954-1982) (José Antonio Márquez). On the right stands the tomb *of Cardinal Manuel Joaquín Tarancón y Morón*, Archbishop of Seville (1857-1862). Several pictures decorate the interior of the chapel.

The stained glass window (28) representing *St. Gregory, St. Augustine, St. Ambrose and St. Jerome* is by E. Alemán (1478-1479).

St. Hermenegild's Chapel. A stained glass window (29) with the symbols of *the Incumbent* sheds light on a simple altarpiece bearing *St. Hermenegild,* made of gold-ground, polychrome wood, who is accompanied by a *Saintly Bishop* and a *Benedictine Saint. Our Lady of Mount Carmel* is portrayed in the attic of the altarpiece. Angels provide the finishing decorative touch to the ensemble (Bartolomé García de Santiago and son, 18th century). The beautifully carved figure by Pedro Millán (1506) standing on the altar can be identified by the garrotte as *St. James the Lesser*. His face has exceptionally noble features, his hands are perfectly formed and his robes hang realistically. This is the only image that has been preserved from the original lantern over the crossing tower that collapsed. The other figure is *St. James the Greater,* dressed as a pilgrim, carved in wood (16th century). Next to these figures are two silver busts with reliquaries engraved on their breast and enamel inlay. They form part of the silver altar that is erected on Maundy Thursday and at Corpus Christi.

In the centre of the chapel stands a truly outstanding work: the *sepulchre of Cardinal Juan de Cervantes*, Archbishop of Seville (1449-1453) and founder of the chapel. It is one of the finest pieces crafted by Mercadante of Brittany. An alabaster catafalque supports the reclining figure of the cardinal clothed in the vestments of his office. His face is the death mask and a hind deer lies at his feet in reference to the cardinal's surname –Cervantes (*cierva* means hind deer). Four angels with coats of arms mark out the corners of the tomb chest and more angels can be seen alongside lions decorating the plinth. The monument was built between 1453 and 1458 and links up with the Flemish and Burgundy Renaissance style. The angels are reminiscent of Van Eyck's work.

A stained glass window (39) by E. Alemán above this chapel portrays *Four Saintly Bishops* (1478).

Chapel of the Virgin of La Antigua: Chapel of the Hispanic World or Our Lady of the Discovery. Christopher Columbus prayed at the feet of this Virgin and devotion to her spread to the New World. This chapel is outstanding for its artistic content and ornamental wealth.

This chapel must have once housed the mihrab, the spot marking the direction of Mecca towards which Muslims pray. The current chapel is a hymn to the Virgin created by two archbishops of Seville. Cardinal Diego Hurtado de

Virgin of La Antigua.

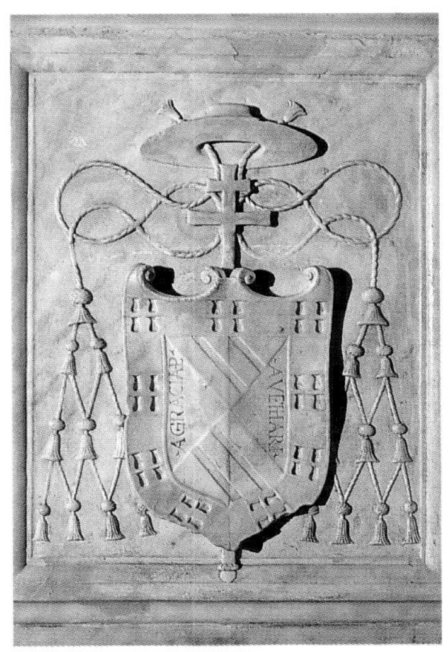

Cardinal Hurtado de Mendoza's coat of arms in the Chapel of the Virgin of La Antigua.

Tomb-chest of Cardinal Hurtado de Mendoza in the Chapel of the Virgin of La Antigua.

Cardinal Hurtado de Mendoza's sepulchre was crafted in Genoa by Domenico Fancelli between 1508 and 1510 when the sculptor travelled to Seville to personally supervise its assembly. He was the first of a subsequently long list of Italian artists who introduced the stylistic language of the Renaissance into Spain during the 16th century.

Mendoza (1495-1502) was responsible for the architecture of the chapel and its interior decoration can be attributed to Luis de Salcedo y Azcona (1722-1741).The Cardinal was so struck by an image painted on one of the walls of the original cathedral that he decided to build a shrine to it. This chapel ended up being the largest of all the chapels and its vaulting only adds to its grandeur. The Cardinal endowed the chapel with generous sums and his wish was to be buried in it. The work was completed by Alonso Rodríguez (1504). The Cardinal had planned –although he did not live to see it happen– that the image and the wall itself would be moved into the chapel. This actually took place during the night of November 7-8th in 1578. The rich decoration in the chapel was paid for by Archbishop Salcedo. He commissioned the marble and jasper altarpiece from Juan Fernández Iglesias and the sculptures from Pedro Duque Cornejo. The stunning image of the *Virgin of La Antigua* dominates the whole space. In this larger-than-life-size fresco painted on the wall, Mary is cradling the Infant Jesus in her arms and she holds a rose in her other hand. The Christ Child is holding a tiny bird in his. Three angels spread their wings out above Mary. Two of the angels hold a crown over her head and the third

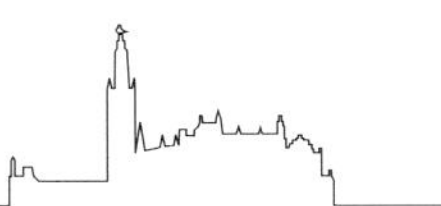

announces a message of hope: *Ecce Maria venit* (Mary cometh). They were restored by Antón Pérez (1547). The tiny figure of a woman prays at the Virgin's feet. The crowns made of gold and precious gems set in the wall were paid for by the local people to mark the canonical coronation (1929). This fine blend of the Gothic and Byzantine styles is dated in the late 14th century and is reminiscent of the Sienna Madonnas. The Virgin is flanked by sculptures of *St. Joaquín and St. Anne. Christ the Saviour* with *St. John the Baptist* and *St. John the Evangelist* can be seen above. Higher up are two symbolic sculptures whilst angels adorn the intermediate frieze. The *tabernacle* is made of engraved silver (Duque Cornejo) and the *crucifix* is marble (Cortezo). The front panels of the altar and the ancillary table, the lectern, the hand rail with the Ave María and the slender angel used for readings, are all made of silver. The two doors of the altar are crafted in ebony with bronze, tortoiseshell and ivory inlay. Huge silver lamps light up the altar.

There are two entrances and two portals leading into this chapel. The largest of the two has an impressive iron screen and was designed by Hernán Ruiz (16th-17th century). The entrance leading into the crossing is an impressive work

Side door to the Chapel of the Virgin of La Antigua with the Pietà Altar on the right.

"The crafting of screens in Spanish cathedrals is certainly not a minor art. It is actually the purest expression of an artistic sensitivity capable of handling forms without making spaces solid (...). Its forms play with the air. They undulate, twist and turn, become rigid in the bars, are repeated with the solemn insistence of a psalmody but, at the same time, they seem to be topped by flowing locks ruffled by a fond Renaissance wind."
(José Camón Aznar)

Virgin of the Elms *in the Chapel of the Virgin of La Antigua. Facing page:* Christopher Columbus' funerary monument.

by Pedro de Riaño although it was actually completed by Martín Gaínza or Hernán Ruiz. The figures adorning this portal are a lesson in themselves.

Right at the top, flanked by two giants and flaming torches, is the *Father*, who decides to save mankind through his son Jesus Christ: *Nativity scene (attic)*; the salvation is accomplished through the Church*: St. Peter and St. Paul*, who appear on either side of the doorway atop green marble columns which may have come from the mosque-cathedral, and the *Six Apostles* around the Plateresque arch.

From their mausoleums the two archbishops keep vigil before the Virgin. The beautifully designed and executed tomb of *Cardinal Hurtado de Mendoza* stands on the right of the altar. The reclining figure of the clergyman dressed in the vestments of his office is framed under a triumphal arch set on piers and six statues: *St. Peter and St. Paul, Two Apostles, St. John the Baptist* and a *Saintly Bishop.* A leafy frieze in relief trails around the tomb chest and *The Resurrection* is depicted in boxes with *St. Anne with Mary and The Virgin Mary with the Child* appear at the sides. In the centre at the top is *The Ascension*. The portrayal of this episode is rather odd as only Christ's feet are visible and the apostles are either seen from behind or from the side. Two female images and coats of arms accompany the inscription on the catafalque. This magnificent work executed in white marble by the famous artist Domenico A. Fancelli di Settignano (1508-1509) was crucial in introducing the Italian Renaissance to Spain.

Very little can be said about the *tomb-chest of Archbishop Salcedo* except that it is a copy of the previous one by Pedro Duque Cornejo (1734-1741). A rounded arch, six statues of saints next to the columns and on the catafalque scenes relating to the Virgin Mary in relief: *Annunciation, Visitation and The Apostles next to the Virgin's grave. The Assumption* tops the whole ensemble. Although it is certainly well-executed it cannot match the Cardinal's sepulchre. The canvases with scenes concerning Our Lady of La Antigua and including the moving of the wall (Domingo Martínez) that decorate the chapel date from the time of Archbishop Salcedo too. Both the chapel structure and its decoration –which was in a poor state of repair– were restored in 1991-92. Today it is the Blessed Sacrament Chapel and is set aside for prayer.

Altar of the Conception. A magnificent pictorial altarpiece by Luis de Vargas (1561) symbolises the genealogy of the Saviour: the human race springs from Adam and culminates in Jesus who is in Mary's arms. Adam's leg (*"gamba"*) in the foreground gives rise to the popular name for the altar. The story goes that the Italian artist Alesio, responsible for the huge St. Christopher opposite, once said*: "Piú vale la tua gamba che il mio San Cristófofo"* (your leg is worth more than the whole of my St. Christopher). Also by the same artist are the *Allegory of the Triumphal Church* which can be seen on the altar and the donor, *Canon Juan de Medina,* and his coat of arms on both sides. The iron screen, designed by Hernán Ruiz and completed by Pedro Delgado (1562), is magnificent.

Altar of the Descent from the Cross or Pietà. Here is another equally impressive pictorial altarpiece. It was painted by Alejo Fernández (1527) and marks the changeover in style from the Gothic to the Renaissance. The central panel depicts the *Virgin next to the dead body of her Son*, accompanied by *St. John, Joseph of Arimathea and the three Marys*. In the background, rather tenebrist in style, is *Jesus in the bosom of Abraham* and the *Apparition to Mary*

Christopher Columbus lived in Seville, that great gateway to the Americas, most of the time he spent in Spain after the Discovery. Seville was also his final embarkation point in 1505 when as a defeated, ill man he made a final attempt to recover royal favour. His mortal remains suffered similar vicissitudes. They were moved from Valladolid to Seville and then on to Santo Domingo, Havana and back to Seville again after the Spanish lost Cuba in 1898. All in all, it is now difficult to guarantee today the authenticity of his burial in Seville's Cathedral.

Above: altarpiece in the Chapel of the Sorrows. Right: Our Lady of the Sorrows. *Facing page: view of the Chalice Vestry.*

Magdalene. The Saints appear at the sides. Above is a figurehead spewing out vegetal motifs. Another board painting on the altar is of *Jesus tied to the column*, with portraits of the Donor on either side. The screen dates from the 16th century.

PRINCE'S DOORWAY

Monument to Christopher Columbus. It is a source of great pride to Seville and the cathedral that it was chosen to be the final resting place of the man who discovered America and who was a resident here for a good many years. The mortal remains of Christopher Columbus were brought to Seville in 1899 and were interred in this mausoleum in 1902. Four giant-size mace-bearers in polychrome bronze with alabaster faces symbolise Castile (the figure bears Granada on the tip of his lance), León, Aragón and Navarre and carry the coffin covered with elaborately carved funerary cloths on their shoulders. The mausoleum is designed in the Romantic style so typical of the time and its artist (Arturo Mélida).

The contribution made by Pedro de Mena (1628-1688) to Spanish Baroque religious images was charged with plenty of emotion. His different statues of *Our Lady of the Sorrows* reached unrivalled levels of pathos as shown by the example in Seville Cathedral.

Left: Saints Justa and Rufina, *by Francisco de Goya. Centre:* the Pietà flanked by St. Vincent and St. Jerome, *by Juan Nuñez and, on the right,* Mary between St. Peter and St. Jerome, *by Juan Sánchez de Castro.*

Clock. Made by *fray* (Brother) José Cordero, this immense clock hangs in its Neo-Classical case (1789) above the door.

St. Christopher. On the right-hand wall is the immense fresco portraying the *Saint protector of travellers*. It was painted by an Italian artist known as Mateo Pérez de Alesio who had worked on the Sixtine Chapel. His signature is visible on the rather unusual parrot at the bottom right of the picture (1584). The enormous, albeit perfectly proportioned, dimensions do not detract from the painting's beauty and bright colours.

Stained glass windows. In this wing of the crossing they are: a rose window of *The Assumption* (31) (A. de Vergara, 1536) above the door; on the right, *St. Hermenegild, St. Jerome and St. Eustace* (32) (Maumejean, 1929-1932); *St. Nicholas, St. Martin and St. Sylvester* and the *Passing of the Virgin* (33) are opposite; overlooking the first aisle, on the left, are *Doctors of the Latin church* (34); on the right, *Saints Justa, Rufina, Barbara and Catherine* (35); in the second aisle, on the right, are *St. Leandro, St. Laureano, St. Isidro and St. Florentine* (36) opposite *St. Inés, St. Agueda, St. Lucia and St. Cecilia* (37) (Arnao of Flanders, 1544-1556).

Chapel of the Sorrows. A modern stained glass window (38) forms part of a chapel dedicated to the Passion. *Christ on the Cross* is depicted in the altarpiece (16th century) and a clothed image of *Our Lady of the Sorrows* (Pedro de Mena, 1680) and paintings on the subject of the Passion are on the altar; an *Ecce Homo* can be seen opposite the altar. The most noteworthy paintings are *The betrothal of the Virgin Mary and St. Joseph* (Valdés Leal, 1657) and *Jacob blessing his children* (Pieter van Lint, 17th century). In the foreground is the mausoleum of the *Devout Cardinal Spinola y Maestre*, canon and Archbishop of Seville (1896-1906). This work by Joaquín Bilbao (1912) portrays the cardinal at prayer.

On display in this chapel is the hugely impressive and rather unusual Tenebrae candelabrum that is used in Holy Week services: "This particular one is

Justa and Rufina, Seville's quintessential saints, were sisters who were born in the Roman city, Hispalis, and who lived and died there. They were potters by trade and are now the patron saints of all potters. Circa 287, during Diocletion's persecutions, they were martyred on the orders of the city governor who had accused them of having destroyed an idol.

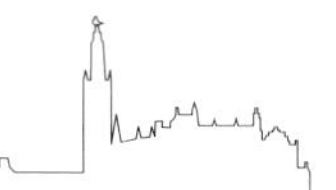

Above left: Lazarus with Martha and Mary. *Bottom left:* St. Peter freed by an angel. *Both works are by Juan Valdés Leal. Above: the tenebrae candelabrum in the Chalice Vestry.*

the best-designed, the most graceful and the most well-made of its kind in the whole of Spain" (Ceán Bermúdez). It was designed by Hernán Ruiz (1559), rises to a height of 7.8 metres and is made of bronze (the base and stem) and wood (the figures topping it).

The stained glass window (39) above the chapel illustrates *Christ washing the feet of his disciples* (Arnao of Flanders, 1555).

This chapel leads into the **Chalice Vestry,** a marvel of soberness and proportion. With its rectangular ground plan (13.7 x 7.8 m), it is one of the most

"It is enough to tell you that its Easter candle weighs 84 *arrobas* [an *arroba* weighed somewhere between 11 and 16 kg] of wax and the extremely grand tenebrae candelabrum is made of bronze and so ostentatious and well-crafted that it would not have cost as much if it had been made of gold." (Luis Vélez de Guevara: *El diablo cojuelo*)

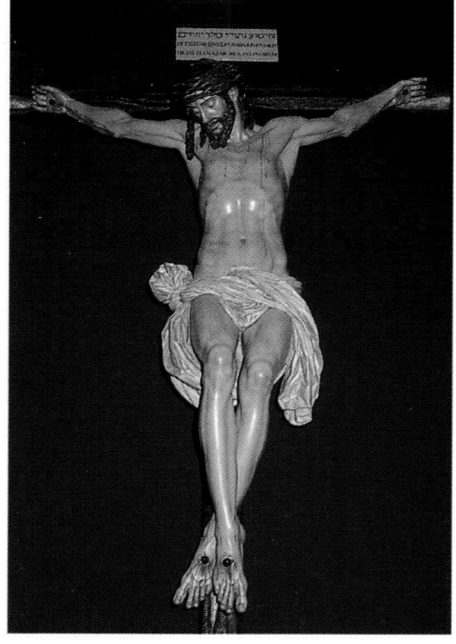

Above: Holy Christ of Mercy *in St. Andrew's Chapel.*
Facing page: Main Vestry.

Designed by Diego de Riaño in 1528, the Main Vestry is one of the grandest works of the Spanish Renaissance period. Laid out in the form of a Greek cross, under a dome on pendentives with fan vaults over the wings, it is a real triumph of the purest architectural Classicism albeit tempered by profuse ornamentation.

successful examples of architecture linking up the Gothic and the Renaissance styles. It comprises a square section and two rectangular sections enclosed by ashlar walling. It has Gothic ribbed vaulting and the corner arches turn into pendentives. The most illustrious architects of that century worked on this vestry: Alonso Rodríguez, Juan Gil de Hontañón, Diego de Riaño and Martín de Gaínza. From the back of the vestry there is access to two oratories. A simple, elegant coffer holds a selection of immortal works.

Saints Justa and Rufina was painted by Francisco de Goya to fulfil a commission from the chapter. The celestial light that bathes the saints in the painting actually streams in from the window on the right; in the background is the Guadalquivir river, the cathedral and the Giralda; the faces of the two simple country girls are turned upwards to gaze at the sky. As well as martyr's palms, they are both carrying bowls in their hands as a reminder that they were potters by trade. The broken pieces of an idol are scattered at their feet. A lion licks St. Rufina's feet. This is one of the immortal Aragonese painter's most perfect religious works. It was painted in Seville in 1871.

The other paintings hanging on the walls are equally important. Above the entrance is a *Crucifix.* On the right, *St. Anne, the Virgin and Child* (Juan Bautista Caracciolo, 16th century); *St. John the Baptist* (Zurbarán, 1640), *St. Peter freed by an angel* (Valdés Leal, 1656), *Holy Trinity* (Luis Tristán, 1624), *The Calvary of the Donor* (Juan Sánchez II, 15th century), *Adoration of the Magi* (Jacob Jordaens, 1669), *The Glory* (Juan de Roelas, 1615), *Our Lady of the Rosary* (Zurbarán school, 17th century), *Guardian Angel* (Mattia Preti, 1660), *The Pietà, St. Vicent, St. Michael and Donor* (Juan Núñez, 1480), *Circumcision of Jesus* (Jacob Jordaens, 1669), *Lazarus with Martha and Mary* (Valdés Leal, 1658), *St. Jerome* (Legot, 1640); *Saints Justa and Rufina*. On the left: *St. Peter* (Pedro Fernández de Guadalupe, 1528), a triptych by Alejo Fernández illustrating the *Birth of the Virgin* (1508), *Presentation in the temple* (1500) and *St. Joaquín and St. Anne's embrace* (1508) and *Adoration of the Magi* (1508), *Virgin between St. Peter and St. Jerome* (J. Sánchez de Castro, 15th century). On show in the two chapels at the back are two ivory crucifixes, an image of the Virgin and a couple of salvers: in the left-hand chapel is the *Paiva Dish,* made in gilded silver, embossed and engraved on both sides (16th century), and the other one was donated by Cardinal Delgado y Venegas (18th century). The display cabinets hold chalices, some of which are made of gold and precious stones, and the *reliquary of St. Millán,* a fretted goblet (Mexico, 16th century).

St. Andrew's Chapel. The figure of *Holy Christ of Mercy* can be seen under a red canopy. It is one of the most beautiful sculptures in the world and the most perfect example of a Baroque Christ on the Cross. This outstanding work by Martínez Montañés is an image of august grandeur that blends religion and art in a perfect body, without a trace of blood, with only the essential marks of the Passion. A shroud tenderly covers his nakedness. The Christ portrayed here is the Christ of mercy and compassion who looks down from the Cross as a saviour not as a judge.

Our Lady of the Fair Wind. This Virgin is the patron saint of ship-owners, captains and pilots working the Indies run and the Mother of so many priests and seminarians who have learnt their vocation at her feet. Juan de Oviedo the Younger executed the figure as a high-relief (1600) and Pedro Duque Cornejo turned it into a statue by adding the wimple, the cloak, the base with its seven

Main Vestry.

"I should not leave the vestry without telling you about Juan de Arfe's famous silver processional monstrance (...). It is unquestionably one of the best examples in Spain and was crafted by the artist with particular painstaking care. It took seven years to complete and its cost, including artistic labour and silver, was said to have been some twenty-five thousand, four hundred and forty-one ducats, six reals and twenty-five maravedies and it weighs ten *arrobas* of silver".
(Antonio Ponz: *Viage de España*)

angels and the clouds. The crowns, crescent moon and the caravel are the work of the silversmith Juan de Garay (1721-1725). The chapel is decorated with a number of fine paintings. Backing on to the chapel walls and the parapet of the screen are four Gothic marble tomb-chests with the reclining figures of three male and one female members of the Pérez de Guzmán y Ayala family. They were originally in the church-mosque and are now the oldest sepulchres in the cathedral (14th-15th century).

A stained glass window depicting the *Last Supper* (40) by Arnao of Flanders, 1555, overlooks this chapel.

Main Vestry and Chapter House. Behind the magnificent wrought iron screen is a vestibule where one of the huge choir books is exhibited. The cathedral actually possesses over three hundred similar books which were illuminated by the leading miniaturists of the time (15th-18th century). On the left-hand wall hangs *St. Anthony* (Zurbarán or his school). The space is almost

Left: view of the dome of the Main Vestry. Right: Zurbarán's St. Teresa, *also in the Main Vestry.*

entirely filled by two huge wooden cupboards with relief carvings of Bible scenes and female figures (Duque Cornejo, 1743).

This vestry is rather more than a room where the celebrants can don their vestments, it is a real church inside the cathedral with its own altar and presbytery. Work began on the vestry under the direction of Riaño (1528) and was completed by Gaínza (1547). The doors are two works of art in themselves. Their relief carving depicts *St. Isidro and St. Leandro and Saints Justa and Rufina* and four medallions with the *Evangelists*; on the other side are *heads of prophets, virtues and cherubs* in hexagons (Diego Guillén Ferrant, 1548-1549). The oblique arch of the Plateresque portal is decorated with caissons depicting plates of food with the meals people would have eaten then. The ground plan is laid out in the form of a Greek cross under a dome and measures 18 metres along the side and 33 metres in height. Columns with carved pilasters ending in an ornamental frieze stand on a rostrum. Above them, three staggered sections in relief tell the story of man's destiny by way of the teaching of the catechism. The lower part shows *the damned* with *Christ the Judge* standing over them, accompanied by the *Virgin, St. John the Baptist, and the Celestial Court*; in the lantern is the *Trinity*, the supreme salvation, whilst the vaulting pays tribute to the *blessed.*

Three altars are situated at the east end of the vestry, with their presbytery. The vault over the middle altar is a relief of the *Assumption* and the other two vaults are embellished with caissons. These altars provide a backcloth for three really unique paintings. The dramatic *Descent of Christ* by Pedro de Campaña (1547) is painted in oil on board. The story goes that Murillo was so taken by this particular painting when he saw it that on being told it was time to go he said "Wait until they finish bringing him down". The other two tiny chapels hold *St. Teresa* by Zurbarán and *The Martyrdom of St. Lawrence* by Lucas Jordán: two

St. Teresa of Jesus arrived in Seville on May 26th, 1575 and stayed in the city for just over a year, setting up one of her most trouble-stricken foundations. That did not stop the Chapter, however, from commissioning what has since become one of the most popular portraits of the saint following her canonisation in 1622.

Above: Juan de Arfe's processional monstrance. Right: St. Ferdinand *by Pedro Roldán.*

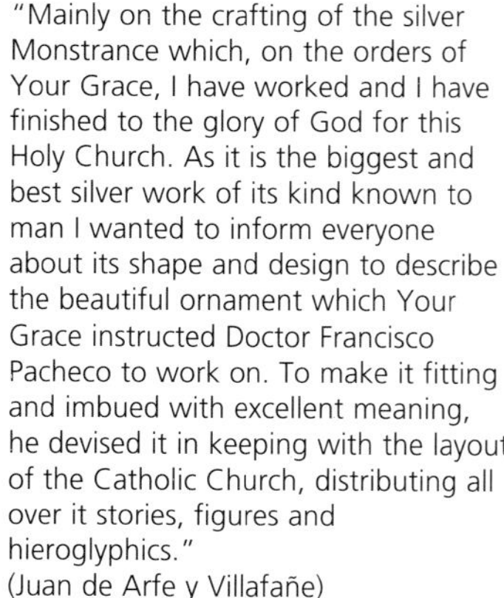

"Mainly on the crafting of the silver Monstrance which, on the orders of Your Grace, I have worked and I have finished to the glory of God for this Holy Church. As it is the biggest and best silver work of its kind known to man I wanted to inform everyone about its shape and design to describe the beautiful ornament which Your Grace instructed Doctor Francisco Pacheco to work on. To make it fitting and imbued with excellent meaning, he devised it in keeping with the layout of the Catholic Church, distributing all over it stories, figures and hieroglyphics."
(Juan de Arfe y Villafañe)

quite exceptional works. These altars held reliquaries until the 19th century and today the items they exhibit are an ivory crucifix, two silver lecterns, effigies of the Christ Child, little angels, paxes, ciboriums and crosses. There is an outstanding *Head of St. John the Baptist*, by Juan de Mesa, carved in polychrome wood (1625). The salver is enamelled silver (18th century).

A number of fine paintings adorn the bare architecture of the side walls: *St. Leandro* is lined up with *St. Isidro*, both works commissioned from Murillo to enhance this vestry (1655) by the cathedral chapter. St. Isidro is totally absorbed in what he is reading whilst St. Leandro holds a sheet that says "Believe, Goths, for he is inseparable from the Father", in reference to the Arrian heresy that he

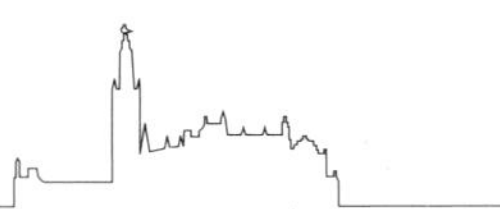

Keys to the city.

fought so tirelessly against. The other pictures are *The Pietà* (Francisco Bayeu, 1788), *Saints Justa and St. Rufina* (Miguel de Esquivel, 1620), *Vision of St. Francis* (Juan Sánchez Cotán, 162), *The apparition of Christ to St. Ignatius of Loyola* (Alonso Vázquez, 1595) and *Our Lady of Mercy* (Juan de Roelas, 1621).

A number of the cathedral treasures are on display here.

In the middle stands the huge monstrance crafted by Juan de Arfe y Villafañe (1580-1587) which is regarded as "the biggest and best silver example of its kind known to man". It is 3.9 metres tall and weighs around 475 kg. It comprises four sections, each one bearing 24 columns and encapsulates a whole doctrine on the Eucharist. The first section holds Ionic columns and represents the militant Church through thirty-six scenes from the Bible and six images of saints who surround our Blessed Lady (originally it was Faith; the Virgin and the vases of white lilies were added later by Juan Segura, 1668). The second section is Corinthian and praises the Eucharist through six bas-reliefs illustrating sacrifices from the Old Testament. In the middle is the monstrance itself holding the Bread of Life and surrounded by the saints worshipped by popular tradition. The third section has columns of the Composite order and symbolises the triumphant church around the Lamb of the Apocalypse with medallions alluding to Jesus' sacrifice, decorated with statues of saints. The last section is also of the Composite order and is the Holy Trinity, the source and destiny of all salvation. The figure of Faith stands at the very top bearing the Christian standard. The minor decorative elements are also significant in terms of the Eucharist: children, birds, small bunches of grapes. Canon Francisco Pacheco came up with the idea for the icons. The fabric cover is embroidered in silk and silver and dates from the 18th century.

Processional image of St. Ferdinand. Seville-born sculptor Pedro Roldán carved this figure in response to a commission from the chapter to mark the

The Almohad dynasty *–al-muwahhiddun*, "those who affirm the Unity of God"– was founded in the mid-12th century in Morocco by the Berber religious reformer Ibn Tumart. It marked the political, economic and cultural height of the Muslim *Isbiliyya*, eclipsed until then by the splendour of Cordoba. But it also marked its end, as ratified on November 23rd 1248 when the *caid* Axataf surrendered the city's fortress to King Ferdinand III of Castile and, possibly, as the story goes, the very same keys that are conserved in Seville Cathedral's treasure today.

Oils Courtyard.

canonisation of King Ferdinand (1671). The processional plinth is made of silver. The figure is carried through the streets to celebrate the Corpus.

Processional image of the Blessed Virgin, known as the "Concepción Chica" or "Little Conception" by local sculptor Alonso Martínez (1658). It is also carried high during the Corpus Christi celebrations.

The *Giants* on display are two of the four candelabra whose name refers to their height. They are made of embossed, engraved silver (Hernándo de Ballesteros the Younger, 1579-1581).

First display cabinet. Six pairs of *silver reliquaries* (Francisco de Alfaro, 1600). *St. Christopher's Reliquary*, gilded silver, with a hexagonal upper part (14th century) and a lower part dating from the 17th century. A cross-shaped Lignum Crucis made of gold, precious stones, enamelling and magnificent cameos. The base is formed by a Pietà, and five gold statuettes and in its hollowed out foot are engravings of the resurrection and the coat of arms of the Donor. Another rather odd reliquary is the St. Clements reliquary, known as "the coconut" because of its shape (both from the 14th century).

Not only did architects Diego de Riaño and Martín de Gaínza leave their imprint on most of the works in the Cathedral executed in the 16th century, such as the Oils Courtyard, but also on many other buildings. As a result, Seville was to lead the way in the Andalusian Renaissance that started in Granada with Gil de Siloé.

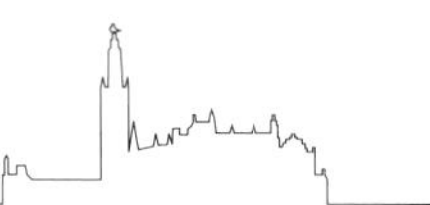

Ante-Chapter House.

Hernán Ruiz II was the most important artist of the splendid architectural school that flourished in Seville during the 16th century. He was born in Cordoba in 1508 into a family of stonemasons. His training was as much practical learning of the constructive techniques alongside his father as it was knowledge of the theoretical works of Italian Classical architecture. In 1557, he was appointed the master builder for the construction of the Cathedral in Seville. He held that post until his death in 1569 as well as carrying out numerous other commissions in the same city and other towns in Andalusia. His best works, however, are to be found within the Cathedral. He designed the Chapter House and the Ante-Chapter House which leads into it, the Former Counting House and the bell tower on the Giralda which was erected over the old Almohad mosque minaret. He also completed the building of the Royal Chapel.

Second display cabinet. *Urns for the Holy Oils* in gilded, repoussé silver (Antwerp, 1564). *Sierpe water ewer* in gilded, repoussé and engraved silver; it has a snake spout, a handle in the form of an enamelled lizard and the lid is a dragon with the globe (Portuguese,15th century). The purple short chasuble, the white dalmatic and the lace alb are examples of the collection of 3,000 vestments belonging to the cathedral including capes, chasubles, dalmatics and so on.

Third display cabinet. *Tablas Alfonsinas.* This Romanesque triptych made of larch wood and coated in gold-plated silver is decorated in gold and precious stones inlay, enamelling and cameos. On the obverse, it is made up of caissons with relics covered by rock glass; on the reverse side, heraldic medallions and reliefs of the *Annunciation* and *Adoration of the Magi*. It weighs over 18 kg and is thought to be the work of the silversmith Juan de Toledo. It was a gift from

Detail of flooring in the Chapter House.
Facing page: Chapter House.

Dome of the Chapter House.

Alfonso X The Wise(1284) and is one of the most unusual and interesting examples of Spanish Gothic silverwork.

Keys to the City. According to tradition these are the keys that King Axataf handed over to St. Ferdinand when he reconquered Seville. The smallest key is made of wrought iron with Arabic inscriptions. The other key is silver with Rabbinical Hebrew inscriptions in monastic lettering.

Fourth display cabinet. The Lignum Crucis with the pectoral cross belonging to Pope Clement XIV. The chapter framed this gift from the Pope in this precious solid gold reliquary. A mapamundi is engraved on the globe using a burin (18th century). A *pectoral cross, a pin and a diamond ring,* a gift from Isabelle II to Cardinal Tarancón (19th century). More pectoral crosses and Episcopal rings. *Four reliquary coffers* by Hernando de Ballesteros the Elder, 1559; another two are by Manuel Guerrero (1730-1740).

Oils Courtyard. A square, inner courtyard or patio, open to the sky, designed by Diego de Riaño and Martín de Gaínza (1529-1537). It comprises three storeys: a series of arches on columns form balustraded galleries on three sides of the patio. The fourth side is the façade wall. Its most striking artistic feature is the verticality of its layout as the only window for light to enter the enclosure is the courtyard opening itself.

Chapter Courtyard or Marshal Courtyard. This is Hernán Ruiz's architecture at its best. It is a square-shaped inner courtyard or patio, open to the sky. The sides of the court are punctuated with walls and windows, some of which are false, and its pediments are adorned with heads (one may be by the same author). An iron railing runs above them (1560-70). Three processional crosses are on display in the adjoining *Column Room*. The Renaissance *Merino cross* is made of gold-plated silver with gold enamelling, cameos and jaspers (Francisco Merino, 1587); the *white glass cross* is actually made of gilded silver, rock crystal and red and green jaspers (Hernando de Ballesteros, 16th century); the third is a gold-plated silver cross.

The stained glass window (41) over the Main Vestry is by Arnao of Flanders (1556): *The expulsion of the merchants from the temple.*

Ante-Chapter House. Entering by way of the Marshal Chapel you come to a quasi-hallway with a stone and jasper doorway ending in a round arch and fanlight and two doors. The left-hand door bears a relief of *Solomon* (medallion) and *Jesus* (rectangle). *David* and the *Virgin Mary* are on the right. The magnificent architecture in this Ante-Chapter House is the work of Hernán Ruiz and Asensio de Maeda (1560-1582). It is laid out on a rectangular ground plan (12 x 6 m), under a vault adorned with caissons ending in a square lantern and with four perfectly symmetrical doors, plus a door leading into the Chapter House. The flooring is black and white marble. A stone bench runs all the way around the room. Great care has been taken over the ornamentation which draws on relief carvings. The tympanums above the doorways portray the *Four Evangelists* and scenes from *Noah and the Flood. Ten episodes from the Bible and allegories*, together with eight figures from the *Virtues* are represented in marble on the side walls, separated by marble pilasters. The decoration is by Diego de Pesquera (1575-1580) with captions by canon Francisco Pacheco. Ceán Bermúdez said of this room that "the antechamber could very easily be taken for a chapter house in the leading cathedrals in Spain on account of its space, its fine shape and its magnificent decoration".

Exterior of the Former Counting House.

Las Gradas (The Steps) was the name by which three of the streets flanking the Cathedral were once known because of the steps that had been built to solve the problem of their uneven ground. *Las Gradas* was a busy, bustling spot in the 16th century where all kinds of transactions - mercantile, banking, unmentionable, criminal and love-related- were carried out in the shadow cast by the Cathedral walls. In 1565, Archbishop Cristóbal de Rojas decided to bring the situation to an end and informed Philip II of what was happening. The response was to be the construction of the magnificent Lonja de Mercaderes which is now the Archivo de Indias and the order was given for the Cathedral to be closed off by surrounding it with chains.

Chapter House. A curved passageway leads to one of the most outstanding spaces in the history of Spanish Renaissance architecture. The jasper doorway is decorated on the inner side with pilasters and a Doric order frontispiece embellished with tiny figures of children (*putti*). The elliptical ground plan measures 14 metres across its longest axis and 9 metres across its shortest. Hernán Ruiz designed it and commenced work on the space (1558) which was subsequently finished off by Asensio de Maeda (1592). The flooring with the same design devised by Michelangelo for Rome's Capitol square is quite magnificent. The space is split up into a number of clearly defined areas. The lower part or seating area is presided over by the *Archbishop's chair*, made of inlaid mahogany and adorned with three small sculptures. In front of the chair is a *secretary's desk* (Diego Velasco, 1529) and running around the whole room is a stone bench with a cushioned covering. A Doric entablature borne by angels runs around the room above this section and under a surround decorated with *eight allegorical paintings* with captions, including *Giraldas and vases of white lilies*, is the coat of arms of this cathedral and its chapter (Pablo de Céspedes, 1529). The second section or storey incorporates Ionic order half columns framing the high-reliefs. The eight largest reliefs deal with the following subjects: *Assumption of the Virgin* (at the centre); on either side of it are *The Smoke of the Abysm and Christ, The Witness emerging amidst the candelabra, Expulsion of the merchants from the temple* and *Allegory of the Final Judgement*. Above the door is the *Mystical Lamb* flanked by *Angels with trumpets* and *Angel with legs as columns of fire*. They were carved by Juan Bautista, Vázquez the Elder, Diego de Pesquera and Diego de Velasco (1582-1584). The content of the smaller reliefs start with the *Assumption, Christ's last sermon, Daniel amidst the lions fed by Habakkuk, Storm on the Sea of Galilee, The Sower, Praying in the garden, St. Peter's Vision* and *Christ washing his disciples' feet* (Marcos Cabrera). The reliefs are interspersed with various Latin inscriptions in gold lettering on dark marble (Francisco Pacheco). A coffered vault springs out of the entablature of this section. The vault is divided into three concentric ellipses with seven round windows (oculi) which, together with the lantern, are the source of the light that filters into the room. The vault is an anthology of Murillo's paintings (1667). One of his loveliest images –the Blessed Virgin– takes pride of place. Eight saints (considered to be) from Seville are portrayed in a circular format: *St. Hermenegild, St. Ferdinand, St. Leandro, St. Isidro, St. Laureano, St. Justa, St. Rufina and St. Pius*. The coat of arms of the chapter is repeated again in the rest of the vault (Pedro de Medina Valbuena, 1668). The vault terminates in an elliptical lantern set atop Corinthian columns. The chapter's task is inscribed on a cartouche at the entrance: *Provide choir and altar*.

St. Joseph *by Pedro Roldán.*

Former Counting House. Known as such because the administrative functions of the cathedral used to be housed here. Entry to this space is by way of the same hallway as the Ante-Chapter House. It has a trabeated portal with an attic (Hernán Ruiz, 1560) and a rectangular ground plan (11 x 7 m). The ceiling is coffered with caissons and gilded pineapple shape elements. This room is used to exhibit many of the cathedral's treasures. In the centre is the so-called *"Little" Monstrance* (Custodia Chica), otherwise known as the *Monstrance of the Holy Thorn*. This Renaissance-style engraved and embossed silver piece (Francisco de Alfaro, 1600) is taken through the streets in a procession to celebrate the Corpus. On display too is the wooden *Model of the Custodia Grande or Large Monstrance* which was given to the chapter by Juan de Arfe in 1580.

The contents of the display cabinets are as follows. On the right of the entrance, **first display cabinet**: *precious monstrance*, made in gold and inlaid with diamonds, two thick pearls, emeralds and rubies; the work of the Sevillian craftsman Ignacio Thamaral (1729). *Large monstrance*, in gold-plated silver, inlaid with emeralds, diamonds and 1500 pearls in clusters; an Italian Baroque work (1778).

Philip V of France's pax.

Patron Saints Justa and Rufina.

"Consecrated to eternity; to the great mother liberator; to the pontiff saints Isidoro and Leandro; to Hermenegild, the happy pious prince; to the virgins Justa and Rufina, with their chastity intact and their manly perseverance, incumbent saints; this African-built tower of admirable sorrow, erected before two hundred and fifty feet, whose costly repair was taken care of by the Chapter of Seville's Church thanks to the favour and encouragement of the highly pious prelate Fernando de Valdés." (Francisco Pacheco, 1568)

Second display cabinet: *urn for the Maundy Thursday ciborium*, made of gold and gold-plated silver (Luis Valadier, 1771), together with *two keys on gold chains* for it (1807). *Gold thurible and censer* (Antonio Méndez, 1791). *Gold altar cruets*, Mexican. Embossed silver *salver*.

Third display cabinet: two *amphorae*, a *jug* and a *salver* in embossed silver.

Fourth display cabinet: Gothic *Alfonsine cross and candlesticks*, in gilded silver, embossed and engraved (1486-1502). Pax designed as a tiny altarpiece, made in gold with precious stones and an enamel figure of the Virgin (16th century).

Pride of place in the room goes to a beautiful carved image of *St. Joseph* in polychrome wood by Pedro Roldán (1664).

Fifth display cabinet: *processional crowns for the Virgen de los Reyes and the Christ Child*. Made in Seville for the canonical coronation, they are crafted in gold and encrusted with pearls, diamonds and precious gems. Gilded, embossed silver salver.

Sixth display cabinet: *cross-reliquary* in gold, enamel and precious stones. A pair of *paxes* with the Ascension and the Assumption made of gold-plated, engraved silver (Ballesteros the Elder, 1556). *St. Anne's pax* is made in gilded, engraved silver (16th century). The other *pax* is shaped like a gold, enamelled shrine enclosing the Virgin and Child inside and with Philip V of France and Jeanne of Burgundy on the doors (Paris circa 1320). *Dish-salver* with the coat of arms of the chapter in gilded silver (Vicente Gargallo, 1700).

Seventh display cabinet: silver *altar cross* (15th century). *Lignum Crucis cross-reliquary* (16th century). *Reliquary of St. Clement*: a golden chalice in which the cup part is a huge agate crowned by the gold figure of St. Clement (1516).

Eighth display cabinet: *two goblets with their plates*, engraved silver (Mexico, 18th century). *Maundy Thursday ciborium*, made in gold and inlaid with diamonds, emeralds and rubies (18th century). Embossed, engraved silver *salver* with gilded decorative elements and a coat of arms (1778). Gold and diamond chalice.

Bust of St. Rosalie in embossed, engraved silver, weighing 42.25 kg (Antonio L. Castelli, Palermo 1681). Donated by Archbishop Palafox in 1688.

Mariscal (Marshal) Chapel. "One of the church's most illustrious treasures that only adds to its grandeur" (Gestoso). Classicism and beauty rule here. If the screen with the *Holy Burial* is an impressive work (M. de Gaínza and Pedro Delgado, 1555), the stained glass window depicting *The Betrothal of the Virgin and St. Joseph* (Arnao of Flanders, 1556) is of an equally high standard. They also serve to enhance the beauty of the altarpiece paintings (1555-1556). The *Purification of Mary* in the centre is one of the most outstanding works from the Spanish Renaissance period although the artist (known as Pedro de Campaña in Spain) was actually a Flemish artist, Peter Kampeneer, who worked in this church. The composition is quite perfect and the female faces so reminiscent of Rafael Sanzio's are magnificently painted. The robes worn by the characters and the colours used only enhance the overall effect. Other equally fine works can be admired on top of the altar*: the Infant Jesus disputing with the doctors,* flanked by *groups of portraits of the Donor and his family*, with their clear Flemish influences. The other paintings are *St. Ildefonso's vision, St. James, St. Dominic and St. Francis*, with their slight resemblance to Michaelangelo's prophets in the Sixtine chapel. A *Resurrection* is hung in the attic under a *Calvary*. The altarpiece

Detail of Marshal Chapel.

was commissioned from Peter Kampaneer by marshal *(mariscal)* Diego Caballero, after whom the chapel takes its name.

EAST CHAPELS

Inside the chapel, on either side of the door, is a painting of *St. Roque* (A. de Alfián).

Altar of the Patron Saints. A quintessential Sevillian sculptural group formed by *Saints Justa and Rufina with the Giralda* (Duque Cornejo, 1728): two pretty girls seem to be holding up, caressing and protecting the symbol of the city. This altar is carried through the streets in the Corpus Christi procession.

Altar of St. Barbara. An altarpiece is formed by ten interesting paintings by Antonio Rodríguez (1545): *Holy Family with an angel offering grapes to the Child;*

"Flemish-born Maese Pedro de Campaña [Peter Kampaneer] was a prestigious painter and a disciple of Rafael de Urbino. He spent twenty years in Italy, studying in that Athens of Painting and showed just how much he had learnt there. He was in Bologna when that great city set about adorning itself to receive the undefeated Emperor Charles V and celebrated his coronation in 1530 when Maese Pedro built a famous triumphal arch which brought him fame and was of great utility to him as he was just twenty-seven years old at that time. After a few years, he came to Spain and stopped in Seville where he crafted some immortal works, especially the Marshal Chapel screen at the entrance to the Chapter House of that Holy Church. And above all, that graceful Purification panel in the chapel of the same name, so famously crafted by his hand."
(Antonio Palomino: *El Parnaso Español Pintoresco Laureado*)

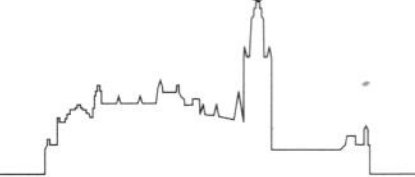

Above: banners in the Royal Chapel. *Right:* Virgin of the Kings. *Facing page: view of the Royal Chapel.*

The Virgin of the Kings is thought to be French in origin, a gift given by St. Louis to his cousin Ferdinand III. It is made out of larch wood but only the face and hands of the Virgin and the head, legs and feet of the Child are carved and polychrome. The rest of the ensemble is a kidskin-covered frame which used to be concealed by the clothing. Inside was a rather odd mechanism –no longer working today– that gave the figure articulated movements.

above it is *Pentecost* and on either side various *saints* including *St. Barbara*. The chapel is also known as *San Antonio* Chico (*Little St. Anthony)* because of the image of St. Anthony it also contains.

Above Campanilla Doorway is a stained glass window portraying *St. Christopher* (42) (Arnao of Flanders, 1546).

Chapel of the "Large" Blessed Virgin. The chapel saint used to be St. Paul as testified by the interior stained glass window illustrating the *Conversion of the Apostle* (43) (Arnao of Flanders, 155). The magnificent altarpiece with its spiral columns (Francisco Dionisio de Ribas and Martín Moreno, 17th century) bears a lovely polychrome wood image of the *Blessed Virgin* in the centre, accompanied by *St. Joseph, St. Paul, St. Gonzalo and St. Anthony of Padua*. The *Crucifix* belonged to the former chapel (16th century). *God the Father* surrounded by the virtues and angels is up above; the carvings are by Alonso Martínez. A marble slab on the left commemorates the Sepúlveda family who dedicated this chapel to the Blessed Virgin. The iron screen bears the family coat of arms (1654). The *sepulchre of*

P·E·R·M·E·R·E·G·E·S·R·E·G·N·A·N·T

Dome of the Royal Chapel.

"The dome [of the Royal Chapel] rises up on the entablature. Placed in the caissons of its coffered ceiling are the heads and shoulders of the kings of Castile with several heads of seraphs in the section descending to the ring. The lantern is decorated with pilasters and its height from the flooring is calculated to be some one hundred and thirty feet."
(Antonio Ponz: *Viage de España*)

Cardinal Francisco J. Cienfuegos y Jovellanos (1824-1847) stands up against the right-hand wall. The tomb-chest with the reclining figure of the dead cardinal dressed in the vestments of his office stands on a plinth and is decorated with figures of the Virtues, angels and his own coat of arms (Manuel Portillo, 1881). This figure is known as the *"Large" Blessed Virgin (Inmaculada "Grande")* to distinguish it from the *"Little" Blessed Virgin (Inmaculada "Chica")* exhibited in the Main Vestry.

Royal Chapel: Marian shrine of the City of Mary. The remains of St. Ferdinand, his wife Beatrice of Swabia, their son Alfonso X The Wise and other members of the royal family, lay in this spot in the original mosque-cathedral. The history of this chapel is determined by its use as a royal mausoleum. Permission was not given for the royal remains to be moved from here until 1433, under the reign of John II, so construction of the chapel could not begin until that time. Martín de Gaínza designed the chapel and began the work (1541) which was continued by Hernán Ruiz and completed by Juan de Maeda. The notification of completion sent to Philip II by the chapter is dated July 19th 1575. The bodies were transferred on June 13th 1579.

The huge iron parclose (Sebastián van der Borcht, 1755) was a gift from Charles III (1771) and bears aloft the figure of St. Ferdinand receiving the keys to the city in lead coated wood (Jerónimo Roldán). The design of the quadrangular ground plan and its semi-circular apse-like east end was intended to bring to mind the Holy Sepulchre in Jerusalem and the Pantheon in Rome. Eight decorated pilasters mark out seven spaces within the chapel: *Throne of the Virgin* with her escort of *St. Peter, St. Paul and the Four Evangelists*, underneath are *St. Isidro, St. Leandro, Saints Justa and Rufina,* two chapels with galleries whose arches bear medallions with the *heads of Garci and Diego Pérez de Vargas*, companions of St. Ferdinand. The *royal sepulchres* are in the last arches. A frieze of children carrying lances and halberds runs around the chapel. The ceiling is a dome adorned with caissons containing the heads of kings, executed in relief and rising up into a lantern. The most striking element of the decoration are the *Twelve kings of Judah* (entrance arch) and a *theory of sculptures* which seems to reach for the sky as if driven by an inner force (apse). Pedro de Campaña and Diego de Pesquera's imagery was executed by Pedro Campos and Lorenzo de Bao (1571-1574). Sitting on a throne (1806) under a silver canopy *(Per me reges regnant [the kings reign thanks to me])* sits the Lady of Seville, the *Virgen de Los Reyes* (Virgin of the Kings), with her Son on her knees. They measure 1.76 and 0.64 metres). They are images to be clothed, made with jointed arms and hands in carved larch wood and with the visible parts of the body in polychrome. This figure of the Virgin dates back to the transition from Romanesque to Gothic and sums up the majesty of a queen albeit without her severity. The Child has an astonishingly life-like face with a mischievous smile and his hair in ringlets. According to tradition, it was thought to belong to St. Ferdinand who donated it to the cathedral. It always presided over this chapel and the canonical coronation took place on December 4th 1904. There is a relief above the alter with the *Vision of Isaiah* and above it the Heavenly Father. The front panels of the alter and the ancillary tables are made of silver (Villaviciosa, 1739). The two-headed eagle candelabra were made in Peru.

Virgin of the Battles.

The funerary urn contains the remains of St. Ferdinand, recently interred, cleaned and reconstructed. He is dressed in his royal vestments and carries the staff and a sword in his hands. The urn (Juan Laureano de Pina, 1665-1719) was a gift from Philip V and stands on a marble pedestal from the original sepulchre. The sides are inscribed with Alfonso's glowing epitaph to his father in Arabic, Hebrew, Latin and Spanish: "He is the most loyal, the most truthful, the most honest, the most frank, the most vigorous, the most handsome, the most suffering, the most humble, the most God-fearing person and the one who served God best (...), and who conquered the city of Seville which is the head of the whole of Spain...."

The free-standing altar bears a front panel of silver crafted by the Sevillian silversmiths Resiente and Villaviciosa that dates from the same period as the urn. A small crypt under the sepulchre contains the remains of other royal personages and the *Virgin of the Battles*, a seated image of the Virgin (13th century) which used to be carried by St. Ferdinand during his campaigns.

The monumental tombs of Alfonso X The Wise and his mother Beatrice of Swabia are slotted into huge Renaissance niches (16th century). The two marble figures with alabaster faces are kneeling at prayer with their gaze turned towards the altar. They were crafted in 1948 by Antonio Cano Correa and his wife (the figure of the king) and Juan Luis Vasallo Parodi (the queen) to mark the seventh

This tiny figure of the Virgin of the Battles is carved in ivory, the symbol of temperance, and once belonged to Ferdinand III. He used to carry it with him on his war campaigns, fastened to his saddle tree or atop the royal banner. It is known that it was in the royal oratory during the siege of Seville and it occupied the place of honour in the triumphal procession into the city.

St. Peter's confession, *Zurbarán*.

centenary of the conquest of Seville. Two tastefully carved stoups (18th century) are situated at the entrance to the chapel. The choir of royal chaplains, the vestry and a small museum devoted to St. Ferdinand occupy the side chapels.

Two stained glass windows overlook the Royal Chapel: *Evangelists* (44) (1547) and *Jesus with the Cross* (45) (1535) by Arnao of Flanders.

St. Peter's Chapel. An exceptional collection of paintings by Zurbarán dedicated to St. Peter can be admired in a rather austere altarpiece (17th century): *St. Peter, in pontifical dress* is in the centre, flanked by *Vision of the impure animals* and *Repentance*; above is the outstanding *Immaculate Conception*, with *Quo vadis?* (Where are you going?) and the *Freeing of St. Peter;* on either side. Just above the altar itself are three more episodes from the life of St. Peter: *Peter walks on water*, *Handing over the keys* and *Curing the cripple.*; right at the top is the *Heavenly Father* (copy). The two stained glass windows also take the chapel's saint as their subject. *St. Peter bishop* (Arnao of Flanders, 16th century) is above the altarpiece with *Papal attributes* (1784) on the left and on the screen (fray José Cordero, 1780) too. This small-scale museum is completed with other paintings on the subject of the Order of Mercy by Juan Luis Zambrano and two pictures illustrating episodes from the life of St. Peter. The funeral monument of the *Archbishop Fray Diego de Deza* (1504-1523) stands on the left. The figure of the archbishop dressed in the

Francisco de Zurbarán (1598-1664) was born in Extremadura but lived and worked most of his life in Seville where he gained an excellent reputation as a painter of religious themes and produced some of his best works as commissions from many ecclesiastical institutions in Seville.

vestments of his office lies under an arch with a lion at his feet. It was built shortly after his death and was moved here from the College of St. Thomas. The *Almohad door-knockers* from the Doorway of Forgiveness are on display in this chapel.

St. Peter, *by Zurbarán*.

St. Peter dressed as the Pope, *Zurbarán*.

Palos Doorway: Well worth noting is the delightful and rather unusual stained glass window (46) featuring *St. Sebastian* as Charles V with his standards (A. de Vergara, 1535). A painting of the same saint can be seen above the doorway itself (Antonio Alfián, 16th century).

Altar of the Assumption. On both sides of the door, with the Assumption featured in relief in the upper central panel, together with St. Ildefonso and St. Diego of Alcalá (Alonso Vázquez, 1539).

Altar of Mary Magdalene. The most outstanding panel in this altarpiece holding nine canvases on board from the Alejo Fernández school (16th century) is the *Apparition of Jesus to Mary Magdalene* and the *Donors*, and the *Annunciation to Mary* in the second section.

The two stained glass windows by Arnao of Flanders in the retrochoir are *The Evangelists* (47) (1547) and *Jesus with the Cross* (48) (1535).

"Some heads of old men, like the St. Peter in Seville (...), bring to mind figures that Ribera drew so insistently. But the truth is that Zurbarán owes it all to himself. He is unique and stands alone."
(J. Lassaigne)

The Seises dancing before the high altar. Facing page: view of the crossing.

The *Seises* children's choir has close ties with the Cathedral in Seville. The choir has been performing its songs and dances in the Cathedral to mark its most important celebrations since it was set up in 1439. The children's current attire and repertoire date back to the 16th century. Before that they used to sing carols dressed as shepherds and accompanied by tambourines.

A CATHEDRAL WITHIN THE CATHEDRAL

The Chancel is a separate unit within the cathedral, enclosed by a masonry wall with carvings and excellently crafted Gothic fired clay statutes and enormous screens (1522-1575). Work on the enclosing elements commenced under the direction of Miguel Florentín (from 1522), was continued by Juan Marín (1564) and then by Diego de Pesquera (1571). The central section holds a total of 18 statues with 16 at the sides. Pride of place in the central section (opposite the Royal Chapel) is given over to the truly beautiful image of the *Virgin of Repose with the Child asleep on her breast* which used to be devoutly worshipped by local pregnant women. It rises to a height of 1.53 metres and was made by Miguel Perrín (1540). Three statues stand on one side of the Virgin with four on the other side, "because Gothic architects did not seem to be particularly concerned about harmonious proportions." (Ceán Bermúdez).

Chancel screens. Three gilded wrought iron Renaissance screens separate the chancel from the presbytery although they do not block it off completely. Bartolomé de Jaén was responsible for the design of the central screen which is a

Altarpiece in the Chancel.

Almost a century was needed for the work on the Chancel altarpiece to be completed. As a result, the evolution of Sevillian sculpture over that time can be traced in its execution. Work commenced in 1481 with Pyeter Dancart in the Gothic style. In the early 16th century, the brothers Jorge and Alejo Fernández (the former a sculptor, the latter a painter) took charge of the work. The influence of the Italian Renaissance can be seen in this phase. The extension to the altarpiece at the sides, designed by Roque de Balduque in the mid-16th century, is fully Renaissance. When Balduque died in 1561, Juan Bautista Vázquez took over. His style is considered to be the forerunner of the great school of Baroque religious images that was to flourish in the following century.

work by Fray Francisco de Salamanca (1524-1528). Six Corinthian columns on pedestals and bearing relief decoration articulate the grille. The first frieze has open-work ornamentation and angels, with a medallion portraying the face of the *Saviour* at its centre point. *Five prophets* appear on the second frieze and above that is an iron picture representing the *Burial of Jesus* flanked by

Nativity, *altarpiece detail.*

candelabra, flames and little angels. A cross is placed above them. Two pulpits are situated at the sides of the screen on top of iron columns with marble pedestals by the same artists. The two screens at either side of the chapel are the oldest. The pilasters punctuating the screen rise up from low Gothic stone walls and end in open-work friezes featuring flames and candelabra (Sancho Muñoz and Diego de Huidobro, 1518-1523). Two huge silver lamps hang next to these screens.

Altarpiece. Even though it does not merit an entry in the Guinness Book of Records, this altarpiece –18.2 metres wide, 27.8 metres high– is actually the largest surface area of polychrome wood in existence. It is like a giant-size triptych, over which a canopy-baldachin juts out, crowned by a topmost section (beam), with a unique Calvary presiding the whole ensemble. The Flemish artist Pyeter Dancart designed it and was responsible for the initial work on the altarpiece (1481-1488). Master builder Marco, Pedro Millán, the brothers Jorge and Alejo Fernández (sculptor and painter), Roque de Balduque and Juan Bautista Vázquez the Elder carried on where he left off. It was finally completed on January 17th 1526. The sides were added later (1549-1564). Gothic in style, the

The altarpiece underwent thorough restoration in 1979 to save it from the rather worrying state it was in due to the ravages of time and wood-eating insects.

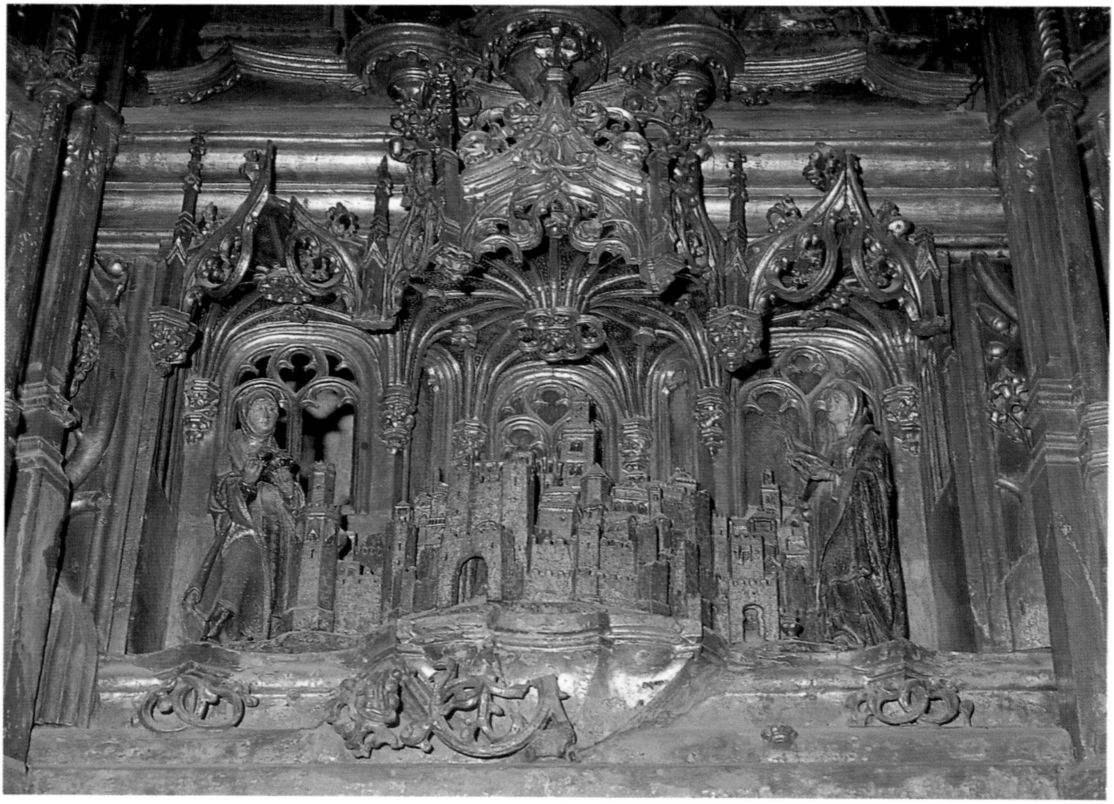

Model of Seville *on the altarpiece.*

altarpiece is carved in walnut, laburnum wood and chestnut. The central part is split into seven vertical panels and five horizontal rows with the lowest panel (containing three sculptural groups with views of Seville) the smallest. Viewed from the bottom upwards, the central panel features*: Nativity, Assumption, Resurrection and Ascension*. The other pictures follow a horizontal sequence, starting at the lower right section with a catechism teaching about the life of Jesus. Further episodes from the life of the Saviour, interspersed with others from the Bible, appear on the sides. There are 44 high-reliefs in all. A total of 189 tiny sculptures alternate on the pilasters and some of them are particularly fine works. The huge baldachin is formed by caissons and crowned by a set of the Apostles with the *Fifth Angustia (Distress)* in the middle: Mary with the body of Jesus and the Holy Women (Jorge and Alejo Fernández). This forest of polychrome wood is topped by the *Christ of the Million*, an image of Christ on the Cross flanked by the Virgin and St. John: "the fine drawing, modelling and carving, together with its composition, polychrome work and holy unction which dramatises the academic naturalism so typical of the middle Gothic period make it a real masterpiece" (José Hernández Díaz). The reason behind its name is unknown. It

"And Seville is the best fortified enclosure of any others to be found or seen on this or the other side of the ocean and that is so flat. Her walls are high and strong and very wide; high towers, well-distributed, large and well-made; any other town would be well-fortified with Seville's barbican alone."
(Alfonso X, The Wise: *Primera Crónica General*)

Left: Our Lady of the See. *Above: lectern on the high altar.*

may have been called that because of the requests that it granted or the indulgences gained by praying to it. Take a good look at the perfectly formed figures including the ones farthest away; the decoration is practically miniaturist in detail. The *Creation* and the *Paradise* by Juan Bautista Vázquez the Elder (1561-1563) are two of the most notable scenes on the sides.

Our Lady of the See. The Virgin after whom this chapel is named presides over the altar in the centre of the lower section. The figure of the Virgin is seated, her beautiful face glows and in her hand she holds a silver-trimmed glass apple; the Child blesses the globe. This work marks the zenith of Spanish medieval sculpture (13th century). It is carved in cypress wood with polychrome features whereas the rest of the figure is plated in embossed, engraved silver. According to tradition, this image used to be placed in St. Ferdinand's camp and was brought back to Seville to preside over the ceremony that converted the great mosque into the Christian cathedral (Christmas 1248). The silverwork is thought to be by Sancho Muñoz (1366).

The Tabernacle. The altar holds the engraved, gilded tabernacle, decorated with columns, reliefs and statuettes and two huge silver lecterns by Francisco de

Although tradition says it was donated by Ferdinand III, it seems much more likely that it was his son, Alfonso X the Wise, who commissioned craftsmen in Burgos to carve the polychrome cypress wood image that presides over the high altar in Seville's cathedral. Its embossed silver coating was added in the 14th century.

Bells on the choir screen.

The Virgin crowning the huge lectern.

Alfaro, (1593-1596). Two sculptures of *St. Isidro and St. Leandro* can be seen in the upper presbytery. Their hands and faces are carved in polychrome wood and their robes are sliver-plated and inlaid with precious gems (1741). They form part of the silver altar. There is also a rather unusual lectern in the form of a kneeling angel who supports the book of readings. This work by Francisco A. Girón is made of gilded, polychrome wood (17th century) and is part of the extraordinary choir used on Maundy Thursday and to celebrate Corpus Christi. In the lower presbytery are the enormous silver candelabras known as the *Vizarrones* because they were a gift from the Archbishop and Viceroy of Mexico Juan Antonio Vizarrón (1744).

Two stained glass windows shed their light onto the presbytery: *Death of the Virgin* (49) and *Glorification* (50) (Jean Jacques, 1511-1518)

Sanctuary: the space between the Choir and the Chancel.

Four triple stained glass windows are set above this part of the cathedral. The two by A. de Vergara are *Presentation, Annunciation and Visitation* (51) (1525) and *Seeking the Child, Jesus among the doctors and Encounter* (52) (1526). The other two are modern (1913).

Choir. The choir fills the space under the fourth and fifth vault and is situated in the nave, close to the Chancel. Three of its sides are closed off by masonry walls and the fourth by a splendid Plateresque gilded iron screen on the theme of the Tree of Jesse. Scrolls of foliage branching out from the stretched out body culminate in Jesus and tell the story of Christ's humanity. Medallions with four apostles are at the sides (Francisco de Salamanca, 1518-1523). The choir measures 20 m x 14 m. The choir stalls are a real jewel. There are 117 seats in all, 67 in the upper part and 50 in the lower part. They are made in the Gothic Mudejar style using precious woods. The lower seats feature the inlaid image of the Giralda as it was then. The headrests depict episodes from the Bible in relief and the misericords (the front of the moveable part of the seats) are illustrated with monstrous images of vices and sins. The upper seating is similar except for the arches that rise out of the seats. The arches are held up by 114 tiny wooden statues and over them is a crested canopy resting on 72 tiny figures. The Archbishop's seat and prie-dieu and those of his attendants are particularly fine examples. They are thought to have been made by master Guillén who made the doors of the Main Vestry (1548). In the place of honour reserved for the king, second to the left looking towards the altar, are the coat of arms of Castile and León in marquetry and the inscription "Nufro Sanches, engraver, now with God, made this choir. It was finished in 1478" although it was actually completed by Pyeter Dancart.

Lectern. This huge four-sided lectern in wood and bronze was once used to hold the equally huge choir books. It swivels on a round foot and is decorated with medallions with figures relating to music (Juan Marín, Juan Bautista Vázquez the Elder and Francisco Hernández, responsible for the sculpture and Bartolomé Morel for the casting work, 1562-1565). It is topped by a shrine with the image of the Virgin, a crucifix and the Evangelists (Bautista Vázquez). The huge proportions of this beautiful artefact are not at all at odds with its delicate design and finishing.

Organs. A monument to music and the musicians who brought distinction to this cathedral: Guerrero (1549-1599), Antonio de Ripa (1768-1795), Hilarión Eslava (1830-1847) and Eduardo Torres (1910-1934) to name just a few.

Organ: right-hand side of the cathedral.

St. Joseph *on the choir stalls.*

Construction of these organs commenced in 1724 and since then their mechanism has been brought up to date on countless occasions. There are actually two organs which are double-sided and a single console. The external part including the sound boxes and cornices are by Luis de Vilches (1724-1741).The sculptures are by Duque Cornejo. The organs and their music

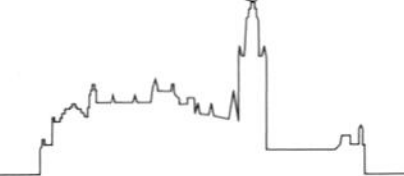

Virgin of Genoa. *Facing page: organ seen from right-hand side of the Cathedral.*

Virgin of the Star.

evoke those heavenly moments when the Seises perform their dance in a tradition which has only been conserved in this Cathedral. Over the eight days immediately following the festivities of Our Blessed Virgin and Corpus Christi, at five-thirty in the afternoon, ten boys dressed as pages and wearing hats dance before the Holy Sacrament o the rhythm of castanets. These age-old dances and songs bring peace of mind and warm the heart of anyone watching and listening. The past blends into the present in their music and their dancing feet.

Four stained glass windows in four openings overlook the choir: *Characters from the Old Testament* (53) (A. de Vergara, 1535); *Kings and celebrities of Israel* (54) (E. Alemán, 1478-1483); *Major prophets* (55) (Zettler, 1908).

Porticoes. Elegant porticoes carved in polychrome marble (Diego Antonio Díaz, 1725) on either side of the choir lead into the Alabaster chapels whose name denotes the material they are made of.

Side chapels.

– On the *right-hand side of the cathedral as seen from the Congregation* are a number of chapels by Juan Gil de Hontañón, 1518:

Chapel of the Blessed Virgin. This tiny space contains a number of exemplary works by Montañés: the *Cieguecita or Little Blind Girl* as it is popularly known (because of her downcast eyes) is the serene figure of a young Virgin who sends out an invitation to pray. She is escorted by the stunningly beautiful *St. John the Baptist Child*, and *St. Gregory*. The reliefs of *St. Joseph, St. Joaquim, St. Jerome and St. Francis* are also by Montañés. Francisco Pacheco painted the portraits of the *Donors* and is responsible for the polychrome of the images (1628-1631). The screen dates from the 17th century.

Virgin of Genoa. Situated between this chapel and the next is an image of the Virgin (73 cm) This Italian polychrome alabaster figure used to belong to an old brotherhood of Genoans living in Seville (14th century).

Chapel of the Incarnation. The *Annunciation* in the centre and the half figures of *St. John the Baptist, St. John Evangelist, St. Dominic, St. Francis and St. Anthony* all belong to the Montañés school. The *Heavenly Father* in relief crowns the ensemble (1630-1635). The Baroque screen commemorates the patrons.

Retrochoir. This section of the cathedral is particularly spacious and well-lit. It takes up a third of the whole length of the church and is lit by the stained glass windows in the nave, side aisles and chapels. The altar occupies the whole width of the nave and is 8 metres high. Its elegant design, different coloured jaspers, bronzes, sculptures and paintings enhance the beauty of the painting on board of the Virgin of Los Remedios, with a saintly bishop and a clergyman on his knees (14th century). This is one of the finest and oldest paintings in the cathedral. Below it is a bronze by Francisco Pacheco entitled *The delivery of Seville to St. Ferdinand* (1633). At the sides are four reliefs dealing with subjects related to the Eucharist and above the secondary doors are busts of Saints Justa and Rufina with various sculptures in the attic including one of a child in the centre (16th century). It was designed by Miguel de Zumárraga and completed by Pedro Sánchez Falconete between 1620 and 1635.

Retrochoir. Facing page: view of the arches in the central aisle, the bays and the stained glass windows from the retrochoir.

The multifarious Mannerist altarpiece that forms the retrochoir was built during the first third of the 17th century with marbles, jaspers and bronzes. Just below it is the tombstone corresponding to Hernando, Christopher Columbus' son who was also an eminent bibliophile.

– On the left-hand side of the Cathedral as seen from the Congregation the chapels are by Gil de Hontañón and Diego de Riaño 1523-1532.

Chapel of the Virgin of the Star. This lovely image may have been made by the French artist Nicholas de León (1539; polychrome, 18th century); *St. Joaquim and St. Anne* are at the sides. The screen is pure iron embroidery, designed by Hernán Ruiz (1568).

St. Gregory's chapel. A polychrome wooden figure of the chapel saint is the centre. The signature of its author, Manuel García de Santiago, appears in the book carried by the saint (18th century). The Plateresque decoration and iron screen date from 1650.

> "Behold the dwelling of God is with men. He will dwell with them, and they shall be his people and God himself will be with them"
> (Revelation 21.3)

This book published by Aldeasa, was printed on
July 24th, 2003, in Madrid, at Estudios Gráficos Europeos